The Mad Chopper

The Mad Chopper

How the Justice System
Let a Mutilator Free,
This Time to Kill

FRED ROSEN

INTEGRATED MEDIA
NEW YORK

All rights reserved, including without limitation the right to reproduce this book or any portion thereof in any form or by any means, whether electronic or mechanical, now known or hereinafter invented, without the express written permission of the publisher.

Some names have been changed to protect the privacy of individuals connected to this story.

Copyright © 1999 by Fred Rosen

Cover design by Gabriela Sahagun

978-1-5040-2310-8

This edition published in 2015 by Open Road Integrated Media, Inc.
345 Hudson Street
New York, NY 10014
www.openroadmedia.com

IN MEMORIAM:
WAYDE PRESTON, DOUG MCCLURE, JOHN RUSSELL,
CHUCK CONNORS AND ROY ROGERS.

A WORD ABOUT SOURCES

The story you are about to read is true. It spans two states and twenty years.

Interviews, official documents, statements to police and reporters, as well as newspaper articles, have all been used in the writing of this book. In the event that two participants offer differing, noncorroborating accounts of the same event, the author has used his journalistic prerogative to choose which version to present.

Dialogue has been extracted from the author's interviews, court documents, Singleton's murder trial, and newspaper articles. Some scenes have been dramatically recreated to portray episodes that occurred. A few scenes might be presented out of chronological order to simplify the narrative. Likewise, the Singleton investigation involved many police officers and for the sake of clarity, the story is presented principally through the eyes of the lead police officers.

The author has chosen to change the names of some individuals to afford them privacy. Any similarity between those fictitious names used and those of living persons or dead is purely coincidental.

I'd like to thank Captain Richard Breshears of the Stanislaus County Sheriff's Office in California, and Vilma Bean of the Hillsborough County Sheriff's Office in Florida for their invaluable assistance in writing this book, and Kensington Editor-in-chief Paul Dinas for his patience and guidance.

The Mad Chopper

PROLOGUE

TAMPA, FLORIDA
FEBRUARY 9, 1997

The 911 call came through at 6:07 P.M.

"He's beating a woman, he's beating a woman," the caller said frantically.

"Where is this, sir, and—"

"Listen, we just went up to the house and there was this guy inside and he was beating this woman."

"What's your name, sir?" asked the operator, speaking in the rational tone she had been trained to use when someone half crazy with fear called.

"My name's Gene Reynolds. And it's that guy, that guy—"

"What guy sir? Take your time, just calm down." Her training included calming people down when they were excited.

"Okay, okay," and Gene slowed down a little. "Okay, now I don't know what the deal is, but the person that lives in that house is the same guy that cut that girl's arms off, that fifteen-year-old in California."

The operator didn't know what the hell he was talking about, but she still didn't have an address. After Reynolds gave it to her, she said the police would be there immediately. That was another thing 911 operators were trained to do. Say that the cops would be there immediately.

Hillsborough County, of which Tampa is a part, claims that the average response time to emergency calls is 9.1 minutes. It took thirty-four minutes for the first police car, with one Hillsborough County deputy, to arrive at the address. The cops would later explain the delay by saying it was "shift-change time and it was rush hour traffic." Besides, no matter how fast they had arrived, the girl would have been dead anyway. Or so they would claim.

The murder had occurred in Orient Park, a neighborhood best described as the armpit of Tampa. Rundown, one-family houses lined the narrow streets, but the one Deputy Paul Robbins stopped at was nicer than the rest. It looked as though someone had put a lot of money into renovating it.

Robbins didn't know it, but he was right. Ninety grand had been sunk into what had once been a rundown bungalow to make it what it was now, a jewel of a house, the nicest in the neighborhood, which literally shone in the blue light of dusk. But Robbins didn't really care about its appearance. His eyes were trained on the vicious-looking Rottweiler that was guarding the door. It wasn't on a leash and it was barking its head off.

Stu Simon, who lived across the street, heard the barking and came out on his porch. He saw the dog barking and the police car parked in front of the house and immediately knew it was big trouble. Stu quickly walked across the street.

"I'll tie Kayla up, officer," he said and approached the dog without any fear He tied her to the front fence and turned back to the cop.

"We have a report of a domestic disturbance here," said Robbins.

Stu went up to the front door and knocked without hesitation.

"Bill, the law's here," he said and knocked again.

The door was answered by a naked man covered with blood and wearing a condom. He was staggering as though he was drunk. Before he could say anything, the phone rang. He didn't seem to hear it. *Bill always responded quickly to phone calls*, Stu thought "Bill, the phone's ringing," Stu said gently.

The naked man went back into the house to answer it. Hand on his weapon, Robbins hesitantly followed him.

On a sofa at the other side of the narrow room the deputy saw the body of a woman. He went over to look and saw that she was covered in blood. She was dead. He looked up. The naked man was standing over him. He had a mournful look on his face and he said nothing.

"What happened here?" Robbins asked.

The man still said nothing. Robbins reached to the back of his belt, pulled off his cuffs, then spun the guy around.

"You're under arrest," he said, then added, "for murder."

There was no need to frisk him.

PART ONE
THE MUTILATION

ONE

BERKELEY, CALIFORNIA
1978

The University of California at Berkeley is situated across the bay from San Francisco. A hotbed of radicalism in the 1960s, Berkeley, as the school was commonly known, clung to its radical reputation in the 1970s like a baby to its bottle.

The reputation fed the school's popularity and as such, its radical past, and present, provided a haven for those free-thinking academics who would have found it difficult to teach at most other universities. Students knew this, and those who wanted to be taught in a different way, free from the rhetoric and mores of contemporary society, still flocked to Berkeley. Enrollment was also helped by the fact that it was a great party school.

There weren't too many places more interesting than the San Francisco Bay area. The heavy gay population, and the strip clubs that dotted the landscape contributed to the feeling that San Francisco was a place where you could and would find anything and everything. At Berkeley itself, drug use was still de rigueur if you were a student, and sexy—well, all you had to do was look around at the sun-kissed bodies of men and women in tank tops and shorts, and if you didn't get turned on, then you were surely asexual.

This casual attitude toward sex, and the free-form education structure, contributed to an attitude of permissiveness that blanketed the campus. The last thing on anyone's mind was danger. How could it be, if you spent most of your time partying? But in Berkeley, there was a corner where crime, major crime, was just waiting to happen.

The students called it "Hitchhiker's Corner" on University Avenue. It was the place you went to in order to hitch a ride anywhere in the state. Often it would be a student who'd pick you up. But there wasn't anything to stop anyone else from driving there, someone who wanted to take advantage of, say, some young coed, or some runaway who happened to float into Berkeley. Luckily, nothing major had ever happened that anyone could remember.

Sure, maybe some kid had gotten picked up by some weirdo and been roughed up a bit, and maybe some poor girl had been picked up by some frustrated suburban husband who had forced himself on her. But for the most part, everyone who didn't have a car just hitched and didn't think twice about his or her safety.

Soon, they would.

SEPTEMBER 30, 1978

In Rome, the Pope had just died. The College of Cardinals was meeting to anoint a new Pope. In Northern California, Mary Vincent was hitchhiking.

Vincent was a fifteen-year-old teenager with a troubled present. She had a "companion," twenty-six-year-old Diego Montoya, who had been arrested the previous month on a charge of raping another fifteen-year-old girl in Sausalito. Mary relied on Diego, and with him behind bars, she just didn't know what to do. Her solution was to try to help her friend. Maybe she could help find a way to get him out. Toward that end, Mary traveled to see his lawyer at the Marin County Civic Center.

There, Mary spoke with Diego's attorney. It didn't do any good. Unsuccessful at resolving her friend's legal problems, and therefore her personal ones, Mary needed to find a way to live. She applied for emergency public housing. That didn't work either. Finally, with her options for survival dwindling, with no place to go and no way to support herself, she placed a long-distance phone call to her grandfather, Ricker Vincent, in Los Angeles.

She said that she was coming down to visit him, and asked him to get some money. Mary had little or no money in her pockets, which was why she had to hitchhike to Los Angeles.

Beginning her trek in San Rafael that morning, she was first picked up by a man who was alone in his car. He drove her north across San Pablo Bay on Highway 37. He dropped her off someplace around Vallejo, but not before giving her written directions on how to get to Los Angeles.

Next, she was picked up by a woman who had two men and a dog with her. Traveling south and west on Interstate 80 for approximately fifteen miles, the woman left her off at Hitchhiker's Corner in downtown Berkeley.

Wearing a light pink top, blue jeans, and white tennis shoes, carrying a green backpack and reddish-purple knit purse, Mary looked like the archetypal Northern California—Berkeley hippie. She waited at Hitchhiker's Corner with her thumb out for someone to stop and pick her up. Someone did. A burly-looking guy, with a bulbous nose, driving a blue 1974 Ford Econoline van.

"I'll give you a ride where you're going, if you'll help me load my van at my house," the guy said.

He was vague about where that was, but said it was somewhere "nearby." Mary agreed and off they went.

"My name's Larry," he said.

"I'm Mary."

They drove for a while, up toward the north bay area, until they got to his house, a neat little clapboard number. Mary helped him load up the van with his stuff and once again, they were off.

"You know, I have a daughter," Larry said wistfully. He did not say that he had been accused of beating her, and that his daughter had little or no contact with him, a fact that hurt him deeply.

Mary listened to the man talk about his second home in Nevada, and other facets of his life. After a while, the man's conversation turned boring and ran out of steam. Just as they hit the freeway, Mary dozed off.

It was hard for her to measure how long she had been asleep, but Mary reckoned later it was just a catnap. Yet when she awakened, it was to a tremendous shock.

Instead of being greeted by the lights of the San Francisco Bay area, Mary awoke to see that they had passed Sacramento and were on their way east to Nevada, not south to Los Angeles.

"Hey, you're going in the wrong direction," Mary shouted.

"No, I'm not," Larry answered reasonably.

Whatever he was up to, he tried to stall, to make Mary believe that they were on the right route. Mary, though, was too bright for him and repeated her protest: "Los Angeles is in the other direction!"

Larry stopped the van and forced Mary into the back. Mary was a feisty girl. She picked up a stick from the floor of the van and whacked the man with it. Suddenly ashamed of his conduct, Larry backed off.

"I apologize for my behavior," Larry said sheepishly. "I'll take you where you want to go."

Driving south on Interstate 99, he pulled in at a greasy spoon, in the Sacramento area, where they both got out to get something to eat. Considering the guy's strange behavior, Mary would have been smart to escape from the stranger at that point, but she was clearly not experienced enough and decided to travel on with him.

After the meal, the guy headed out onto Interstate 5 and turned south, toward Modesto. It was a round-about way to get back to San Francisco, but Mary was still not suspicious.

At the greasy spoon, the guy had bought a soft drink. As he drove, he drained some of it and then pulled a bottle of whiskey out from under his seat. While driving, he uncorked it, filled the soft-drink container to the brim with the booze, and continued to drink.

A short time later, outside Modesto, he had found the way into Del Puerto Canyon, a barren, deserted landscape, so isolated it might have been on the far side of the moon. The night was pitch black, and the only sounds were cicadas clicking in the darkness. The sky was like black velvet with diamondlike stars set upon its surface.

Larry put his foot on the brake.

"I gotta go take a leak," he said and pulled over.

"Well, I gotta go do that myself," said Mary.

They both got out of the car to heed nature's call. Mary was just about to take down her pants when Larry came up behind her. He knocked her senseless and then dragged her into the back of the van.

Screaming, trying to resist, but powerless against the man's massive strength, Mary was forced to the floor of the van. Larry loomed over her like some monster, powerful shoulders and chest flexing, rough, callused hands holding her down. He seemed to get off on the power he had over her. He brutally raped her.

Afterward, to show he wasn't all bad, he gave her a drink of whiskey. More likely, he was trying to calm her down just in case she screamed and someone nearby happened to hear her.

Drained, Mary expected that the worst was over when the guy started up the van and drove farther into the canyon. She figured he was looking for the way out. But he wasn't and she knew that when he pulled to the side again.

Her worst fears were realized when he pulled her out of the van and raped her again, only this time, he wasn't content to merely force himself on her sexually. Larry put his hands around her throat and began to squeeze, harder and harder and harder, squeezing the life out of the poor, defenseless fifteen-year-old, who happened to be hitching at the wrong place at the wrong time.

Suddenly, Larry stopped and looked down at her. The girl seemed dead, and his hands were around her throat. He had killed her. He had to think fast.

Larry carried her back into the van. He drove farther into the canyon and then stopped beside a drainage pipe. The pipe ran under the two-lane road. It was a good place to stash a body. Chances were, the girl was one of those troubled runaways whom no one ever missed.

But wait a minute, Larry thought, what if someone did discover her? Yeah, you always had to think about the "what ifs" if you were a smart dude. Larry thought of himself that way.

He was smart all right. Hadn't he chosen to rape the girl in an isolated, out-of-the-way canyon where no one else was around? Hadn't he figured out how to get rid of her after he killed her? But he came back to that question of discovery. And fingerprints. If the cops did find the girl, her fingerprints would identify her and then maybe they could figure it all out.

Fingerprints. Get rid of the fingerprints and no one could identify her. No one could get to him. He'd get off scot free.

It was the booze talking, but Larry didn't know that. Or didn't care. No matter. A plan had formed in his mind and Larry was nothing if not thorough.

Larry hit the brakes. The van coasted to a stop. By this time, he was so far into the canyon, the blacktop had ended and a dirt road had taken its place.

He jumped out, the door closing with a crash, and he went around back to take the body out. He reached in with one arm and draped the body over his shoulder, and with the other, reached under a tarp and took out a hatchet.

Mary opened her eyes and groaned. From that moment on, Mary Vincent was fully conscious and understood everything that was happening to her.

Now he really had to kill her. Otherwise it was prison for raping her. But he had to remember about the prints. The prints. The hatchet.

Larry forced her down onto the gravel, then took her right arm and held it down. He raised up the hatchet and slammed its sharp edge into the flesh of her arm. Not once, but repeatedly until he had hacked off her right arm below the elbow.

Barely conscious, Mary felt the pain and the blood flowing out of her. She felt him spinning her around. She felt the hatchet blade again, this time on her left arm. After several vicious chops, her left arm fell off below the elbow. Mary collapsed from the shock and blood loss and again lost consciousness.

That's good, real good, thought Larry. Without hands, there were no fingerprints. And no identification.

Larry picked her up like a rag doll and tossed her over the embankment. Then he climbed down and pulled her into the ditch and started kicking and shoving her into the drainage pipe until he was satisfied that she was safely hidden. Leaving Mary to die, Larry retrieved the two bloody hands and drove off.

What seemed like hours later, Mary regained consciousness and tried crawling out of the drainage pipe and was almost all the way out before she collapsed again. Weighed down by her body, her bloody stumps were immersed in the cool mud.

Mary had had enough trauma for one lifetime. She needed escape and the only escape available to her now was sleep. Soon her eyes closed and she drifted off.

Larry made his way back west through the San Joaquin Valley, through the San Joaquin Pass, until he got to the Oakland Bay Bridge. It was early, the empty hours of the morning, with little or no traffic. That was why the next part would be easy.

As he drove on the bridge's lower deck, he rolled his window all the way down, and then tossed one arm and then the other out the window. One arm sank in the water below never to be seen again. The other was picked up by the swirling water and carried into an estuary, where it eventually washed up on the rocks.

His night's work done, Larry headed on home.

Mary Vincent lay on the muddy floor of Del Puerto Canyon. Weighed down by her body, the cool thick mud sealed her wounds and saved her from bleeding to death.

As dawn broke, she opened her eyes and blinked, surprised to find herself alive. With the greatest effort of will, the naked fifteen-year-old girl slowly raised herself and walked out of the canyon. The temperature was already climbing into the eighties and sweat poured off her.

All around her was land scorched brown by the sun, eroded by ancient seas until it was unfit for human habitation. Del Puerto Canyon was hell on earth, and Mary had had the bad fortune to be abandoned there.

Suddenly, she heard the sound of cars. Interstate 5 was nearby. That was how they'd gotten into the canyon, she remembered.

Mary took off toward the sound of the cars, following a two-lane blacktop that disappeared over a distant hill. She saw a car approaching over the rise. It began to slow.

"Help me," she shouted weakly.

Seeing this strange, naked, armless girl in front of him, the driver got scared out of his wits. He braked and turned around, speeding away in a cloud of dust, leaving Mary alone again, with little hope of survival.

The sun continued its ascent into the bright blue sky. The heat rose in waves from the blacktop. Mary struggled forward, topped the rise and continued to walk. She was staggering from side to side, her condition worsening by the minute. It was later reckoned by the county sheriff that she had walked a full two miles from the spot where she was assaulted, an astonishing physical accomplishment considering the trauma she had suffered.

It is unclear how much time passed before the second motorist saw her. His name was Todd Meadows, and he was on his way home from work, using Del Puerto Canyon as a shortcut. At first, when he saw her emerging from the shimmering heat waves, he thought her to be an optical illusion. As he got closer, he saw the illusion was in fact a young girl, a teenager, and she was naked. He slowed down as he got to her and stopped.

"Help me," she implored.

Todd got out of the car. That was when he realized that this young, naked girl had no hands! They had been chopped off at the forearm. What was left were dirty, bloody stumps.

Mary collapsed into Todd's arms. He carried her to his car, put her inside and drove. He headed for a nearby air strip. When he got there, he dialed 911. Soon, an ambulance came and transported Mary to the local hospital.

Her assailant's attack had left Mary Vincent in need of surgery. The surgeon amputated more of each forearm so prosthetic arms could be fitted later.

Police made sure that surgeons kept a record of the before X rays. If they ever found the missing hands, they could forensically be matched up to Mary's stumps and used as evidence against her assailant at trial. That is, if there was a trial. The cops had to first catch the depraved son of a bitch who had done this to her. And with a common first name like "Larry," the odds were against it.

TWO

Modesto is the West, in the best sense of the word. In the West, people have a profound sense that justice will prevail. That's exactly how Richard Breshears felt.

Breshears was a tall, lanky young police detective, bright and ambitious, with a studious manner set off by his spectacles. Experienced in different kinds of investigations, from homicides to burglaries, he was assigned the Vincent case as chief investigator.

The newspapers played up the crime's sensational nature. But when you stripped away the sensational aspects of the case, despite the vicious nature of the attack—neither Breshears or anyone else on the Modesto police force could recall such a grisly crime where the victim had survived—it was a brutal case of assault, pure and simple.

While Mary Vincent lay recovering in her hospital room, his job was to find the "bad guy," and that's just what he was going to do. Breshears went to the hospital to interview Mary for any information she could give him.

"He's a merchant seaman," said Mary. "He talked about that a lot."

"Merchant seaman," Breshears jotted down in his notebook.

In relating the events of the night she was picked up, Mary mentioned that the man took her to a house somewhere in the north bay area. "He had a first aid kit that he'd placed in the front window, by the door," she recalled. "He also said that he had another house around Reno."

Mary described what her assailant looked like. Armed with that information, Breshears put out the suspect's description over the teletypes, hoping that they'd get lucky and someone would see Larry or maybe stop him for a traffic violation and arrest him. It sometimes happened like that.

What kind of human being cuts off a young girl's arms? Breshears was determined to catch this guy and put him away for a long, long time. If he could get lucky, or if he worked hard enough, he'd get the guy, and the law would do the rest.

In analyzing the attack, it became clear that it was a pass-through crime, that is, a random act of violence, the kind people always worried about happening to them and seldom did. Mary Vincent happened to be in the wrong place at the wrong time.

Actually, Breshears didn't know where she'd been picked up. That was rather frustrating. Mary said it was somewhere roughly in the Bay Area, but it wouldn't be until his investigation was further advanced that it became clear she had been picked up on Berkeley's campus.

In those early days of the investigation in October, 1978, there wasn't much to go on. The hope was that somewhere, somehow, some law enforcement officer would see the A.P.B. on the man the press called "The Mad Chopper," and identify him. Breshears, though, wasn't going to count on luck or serendipity solving his case. He needed the help of Tom Mack.

Tom Mack was a freehand sketch artist who worked for the San Jose Police Department. His work in law enforcement circles was renowned. Mack relied on his ability as an artist, not the mix-and-match feature kits used routinely in law enforcement.

Mack arrived in Modesto and went to see Mary immediately. Based upon her description, Mack drew a picture of an intense-looking, middle-aged man.

"That looks just like him, as if he was standing there," said Mary, gesturing to the empty space beside her bed.

Breshears had the sketch copied and distributed to police officers, newspapers, and TV stations. The media, meanwhile, had latched onto the story like a leech to a warm-blooded animal.

The Modesto Bee, the local paper, had the exclusive because they were so close to the action, but newspapers up and down the coast sent reporters out to cover the story of the girl whose hands had been chopped off.

Gone from the front pages of the state's papers was the search for The Hillside Strangler, the serial killer preying on the women of Los Angeles County. Now, it was The Mad Chopper who garnered the ink and sent a shiver up and down the collective spine of the state's populace.

Once the wire services went with the story, it became national news, on the front pages of newspapers coast to coast. But no one knew who Mary was, because Breshears and company had to keep her identity secret. Since Mary was underage, she was identified in the media only under the pseudonym of "Maria."

Police agencies in Northern California, of course, were only too anxious to assist in the investigation. No one had ever heard of a crime as heinous as the one perpetrated on Mary Vincent and everyone was anxious that her assailant be caught. It also helped considerably that there weren't many all points bulletins for severed hands.

Across the police teletypes flashed word from Modesto to be on the lookout for Mary's hands.

When Sondra Ruben picked up the paper that morning, the last thing she expected was to see a sketch of her former neighbor, Lawrence Singleton on the front page. But there he was. At least, she thought that was him.

Sondra, a forty-three-year-old housewife, lived in Martinez, one of the small towns that dotted the coastline north of San Pablo Bay. She had previously lived in the nearby town of San Pablo and her neighbor had been a merchant seaman named Lawrence Singleton.

Looking again at the sketch on the front page, Sondra wasn't so sure. The nose was broader in the sketch, the eyes closer to the nose. The lips were thicker and the hairline farther back. Still . . .

She didn't know what to do. The last thing she wanted to do was accuse an innocent man—a former neighbor no less—of such an awful crime. Eventually, she decided to sleep on it. She would take two days before she made her decision.

Breshears had been trained in forensic hypnosis, the science of hypnotizing a person to recall a traumatic, criminal event, in the hope that details surrounding the crime, embedded in the victim's subconscious, would float to the surface. These could then be used to track down the assailant. With few leads to go on, Breshears was ordered by his boss, Lieutenant Chuck Curtis, chief of Stanislaus County Sheriff's detectives, to hypnotize Mary and see what he could come up with.

Breshears went to her hospital room to do the procedure. He explained that there wouldn't be any pain, and she wouldn't consciously remember any of the events. Breshears intended to have her remember the things that happened in the third person, as if they had happened to someone else, and in that way, distance Mary from the event.

Using a pen that he moved back and forth in front of her, Breshears soon found Mary to be a very willing subject. Once she was in the hypnotic state, he began to ask his questions.

"Was the man that picked Mary up, the first person she took a ride with?" Breshears asked.

"No," replied Mary, feeling very relaxed.

"Who was?"

"Another man.

"Where?"

"Someplace in the San Rafael area."

"Describe what happened."

"Mary was picked up by this man," she related as if "Mary" were someone else. "He was alone in his car. He drove her north, around the San Pablo Bay on Highway 37. Before he dropped her off, he wrote out directions on how she could get to Los Angeles."

"What did the directions say?" Breshears was trying to figure out the route Mary took, to pin down where the nut who cut her hands off had picked her up.

"The directions were to take Highway 37 to Interstate 80 to Interstate 5 to Los Angeles."

"And why did Mary want to go to Los Angeles?" Breshears wondered aloud.

"Mary was going there to see her grandfather," the girl answered simply.

"And her grandfather's name?"

"Ricker Vincent."

Now they were getting down to it. Mary Vincent had been hitching a ride to see her grandfather, who lived in the L.A. area, when the "bad guy" got her.

"So Mary was let off in the Bay Area, where she intended to hitch another ride?"

"Yes," answered Mary, relaxing even further into the trance.

"What happened next? Was that when the man with the ax picked her up?"

"No. Somewhere in there, Mary hitched a ride with a woman."

"What kind of car was the woman driving?"

"It was like a Jeep. And she had two men and a dog with her."

"Did Mary talk at all with the woman during the ride?"

"Maybe a little."

"About what?"

"About going to visit her grandfather."

"Where did she drop Mary off?"

"Not sure."

If they could find this woman, she could tell the detectives where Mary was dropped off and therefore, where she was next picked up by the nut with the ax.

"What happened after Mary was dropped off?" Breshears continued.

"Mary talked to a man standing on a ladder. It was leaning against a building, I think, or maybe a roof."

"Can't be sure?"

"No."

"Okay, go on."

"Mary asked him where she could hitch a ride to Los Angeles. He pointed out a place across the street, where some others were hitching."

Mary stopped and thought for a second.

"The man made Mary a sign on cardboard. I think it said, 'Going to L.A.'"

That was all the useful information she could recall. Breshears's boss, Curtis, intended to have detectives cover in a plane the route Mary took for the purpose of identifying the places Mary recalled. In doing so, maybe they'd come up with a lead that would lead them to her assailant.

But time and time again, despite advances in police investigative procedures, despite things like forensic hypnosis, or high-tech searches, cases are solved in the old-fashioned way—with shoe leather.

Breshears knew it was time to take out his walking shoes. Armed with the sketch Mack had made, Breshears and the other detectives working the case hit the road.

There is one fact in any homicide investigation that is not known to anyone but the detectives, the bad guy, and the victim. It is usually a detail, sometimes minute, sometimes major, of the way the crime was committed.

In Mary's case, that detail was her assailant's house. Mary remembered what it looked like and described it in detail to Tom Mack—down to the man's dogs. If they could locate the house, they'd locate the suspect.

During one of Mary's hypnosis sessions with Breshears, she had told him that in order to get to Larry's house, they had to pass over twin highway bridges. Looking at a map, in the area where Mary was picked up, they spotted a town called Vallejo with twin bridges leading into it.

Breshears and his partner, Marc Reese, drove out to Vallejo. They spent five days looking at every single house in the town, trying to match the reality with the description Mary had given them. At night, when they signed in at local motels with their official titles, the desk clerks would invariably ask, "You think that guy lives here?" Everyone was nervous.

Still, it was understandable. To most people, an assault is not palpable unless it happens to them. It's always some other guy who gets hurt by someone who lives outside the community. Then one day some cop stops by, asking questions about a person who could be your neighbor and suddenly it isn't TV anymore, but real life, and you have a psycho in your midst.

Breshears and Reese kept looking, but failed to find the house Mary had described. They personally went to every single newspaper and TV station they could think of, and called every reporter they had ever done business with. The message was always the same: "Please run this picture and this information."

They drove back down to Modesto to get a change of clothes, then headed out again to Vallejo to take one more shot at it. In the car on the way back, they got a call from the office. It was about a tip.

While they were up in Vallejo, the sheriff's office in Modesto had received thousands of tips, from both anonymous and known sources. The department had checked out the ones that sounded reasonable, and had come up with nothing. But there was this one caller who had just called in and she sounded real. It was a woman, Sondra Ruben, who lived up in Martinez.

"I think this guy you're looking for is my former neighbor, Larry Singleton," she told police.

Singleton, she explained, looked exactly like the sketch in the paper, the one the police artist had done. And he had a blue van that looked like the one described in the newspaper articles.

Sondra had moved out of San Pablo a few years before, but the guy in the paper was the spitting image of her former neighbor, Lawrence Singleton. A quick check of the phone book showed that Singleton still lived in the same house.

"He had a daughter and he has a house in Sparks, Nevada," Sondra continued. "And he's a seaman. A merchant seaman."

Everything was fitting, everything was joining together at the seams, Breshears thought. It was hard for him to suppress his excitement. He was like a hunting dog on the scent. He smelled blood.

Sondra gave the cops her former address in San Pablo. Breshears and Reese were traveling in the same general direction as San Pablo. They veered off and took the freeway to the town, which was actually a suburb of San Francisco.

Singleton's address was in a quiet, residential neighborhood, nothing to distinguish it from any other in the Bay Area, or anywhere else for that matter. Pulling the car to the curb, they quickly got out. It was late afternoon, but still daylight. Slowly, they walked up the driveway, and onto the sidewalk. No one appeared to be home.

Sitting on the sill in the front bay window, just as Mary Vincent had described it, was a first aid kit.

This is definitely our guy, Breshears thought. *We got him.*

The front door was locked. They didn't try to enter any other way. That was all they needed—entering without a warrant. With the current liberal bent of the Supreme Court, anything they found, no matter how incriminating, could be thrown out.

Getting back in the car, they drove down to a convenience store they'd passed on the way up. There was a pay phone there and Breshears quickly pulled the receiver off the hook and dialed.

"Let me speak to Don Stahl. This is Breshears," he said into the mouthpiece. Stahl was the district attorney of Stanislaus County. He would prosecute the case when it was made.

"Don, it's me. We're in San Pablo. Look, we found him. We got a tip from someone who saw the sketch in the paper and knew him. Suspect's name is Lawrence Singleton. Call ahead to Sparks and check on his whereabouts over there. Our source says he's got another house there."

Soon the cops in Sparks would locate Singleton's house and descend on him like a blue plague. While that was happening, Breshears and Reese called in the Costa County Sheriff's office. Briefing them on the case, which they knew about from all the publicity, it wasn't hard to get the county sheriff to obtain a search warrant for Singleton's San Pablo house.

Breshears, Reese, and the local cops went back. Armed with their warrant, they knocked on the door, and when no one answered, they broke down the door and entered. The smell assailed them immediately. It was a distinct animal smell, pungent, sharp.

"Dogs," Breshears muttered, "it smells like dogs."

That was it. Mary had talked about Singleton having dogs and how she'd carried bags and bags of dog food out to his van.

It turned out that Mary had given them a fairly accurate description of the house's interior, especially the fireplace. Breshears poked around in the black, charcoal debris that sat in the brick-enclosed space and came up with cloth remnants.

Now, why would he burn clothes? Breshears wondered, and the answer came almost instantly.

He was trying to cover up the evidence. It was the girl's clothing he had burned. Without the clothes, or her body, there would be no evidence a crime had taken place and Mr. Singleton could go on living his life as if nothing had happened.

Peering out their windows, neighbors wondered why, all of a sudden, their block had become police central. There must have been at least twenty police vehicles on the street and twice that many cops, most of whom seemed to be traipsing in and out of their neighbor Lawrence Singleton's house. What could he have done? they asked. He was just an ordinary middle-class, middle-aged man. And so nice. The only time he wasn't particularly friendly was when he was drunk, which seemed to be happening more and more recently.

Inside the house, the "techs" gathered up evidence in their glassine bags, with the detectives supervising. While the house wasn't technically the crime scene, the cops treated it as though it was—vacuuming the rugs, dusting for prints, anything that would help them convict the son of a bitch who had chopped the girl's hands off. There weren't very many cases that raised the hackles on a seasoned cop; the Vincent case was one of the rare few that did.

It was long past midnight when the police concluded their search and took off. For a moment, Breshears gazed at the house, thinking of the girl who had entered with two, whole arms, and the one he knew, mutilated and crippled for life. He was anxious to confront the mutilator. He wanted to see what kind of scum bucket could do such a thing. And he wanted to ask him one question:

Why?

THREE

Lawrence Singleton was arrested at the home of his estranged wife, Celia Johnson, in Sparks, Nevada.

Reporters, who went to the crosstown neighborhood in Sparks, where Singleton lived, discovered his blue van in the driveway of the modest $40,000 tract home. Crime-scene techs were crawling all over it. After they were finished, it would be transported back to Modesto and used against Singleton as evidence at his trial. As for his neighbor's reactions, they were in shock over his arrest.

"He was a peach of a guy," said neighbor Vince Lowell.

"He had this hobby. I'd see him all the time doing it," said another neighbor, Betty Provost.

"What hobby was that?" asked a reporter, hoping it would be something sensational to match the crime.

"Macramé," she answered. "Lawrence made macramé plant hangers."

"And he was quiet," her husband, Scott, added.

I just can't believe it. That was the general response from all of the people who knew Singleton in Sparks. Police told a different story.

"Everything fits," said Stanislaus County Sheriff Lynn Wood. "I think we have enough to put it [the case] together against Singleton." The police relied on citizens to come forward and help, he said, and they did.

In Sparks, police Lieutenant Barry Tone said that Singleton had a police record of minor violations involving alcohol, the most recent a drunk driving arrest on April 30. But Singleton had no record of violent sex crimes, like the one perpetrated on Vincent.

Waiving extradition, Lawrence Singleton was taken back to Modesto for questioning.

Laws may vary from state to state, but interrogation rooms do not: they are always drab, colorless places, smelling of sweat and fear. It was in such a room that Singleton found himself in Modesto.

Singleton was seated at a scarred wooden table. Someone had given him a Styrofoam cup filled with strong coffee, which he gulped intermittently.

Barely over fifty, the years at sea had weathered Singleton's skin and made it the consistency of shoe leather. He looked more like sixty. He was of medium height and stocky, balding, with the veined bulbous nose so common to lifelong alcoholics. His manner was courteous and affable, referring to the cops as "sir," as if to prove that he had been raised the right way, to have respect for the law.

Across from him sat the detectives, Breshears and Reese. On the table in front of them were file folders and a pad, and pens with which to make notes. And in the center of the table was a big, clunky-looking tape recorder. Reese reached over and hit the "record" button.

"Present in the room are detectives Marc Reese and William Breshears of the Stanislaus County, Modesto Police Department. We're here to interview the arrested subject. Could you tell me your full name please?" Reese began.

Singleton looked up. He lit a cigarette and smoke plumed over his head.

"Lawrence Singleton," he answered quietly.

"Spell the last name."

"S-I-N-G-L-E-T-O-N."

"And your home address?"

"826 Glennbrook Court, Sparks, Nevada."

"And your age?" Reese continued.

"Fifty-one," Singleton answered.

"And your date of birth?"

"July 28, 1927."

"Now before we ask you any questions, you must understand your rights. You have the right to remain silent. Anything you say can and will be used against you in court. You have the right to talk to a lawyer for advice before we ask you any questions and to have him present during any questioning. If you cannot afford a lawyer, one will be appointed for you before any questioning is done. You understand all this?"

"Yes."

"If you decide to answer questions without a lawyer present, you may do so. You may stop at any time and demand a lawyer be present before you continue. Okay? Understand that?"

Singleton nodded.

"All right. Now, having these rights in mind, do you realize that we are taping this statement?"

Singleton eyed the tape recorder. "Yes, I understand that."

"This is of your own free will without any coercion or threats on our part?"

Singleton gestured with his hand. He seemed frustrated and answered, "Right, yeah."

"Okay. In your own words, Larry, now, you had talked to me earlier today after being advised of your constitutional rights? Is that correct?"

"That's correct."

"And did you understand your rights at that time?"

"Yes, I did."

"Then, in your own words, why don't you tell us what happened Friday, September 29th, when you left your home to come up here."

"I left San Francisco and went to Berkeley," Singleton began, as though he was describing any ordinary day. "Had lunch around 2:30 P.M. at Spingers and left, and I was going to drive straight to Sparks. I was going home. Anyway, there was a young lady on the on ramp, hitchhiking, so I offered her a ride. She got in and I told her, 'I'm going to Reno. I got to make a stop and pick up some papers and dirty laundry, clothes, and other stuff.' Then I also told her, 'If you'd give me a hand loading that stuff, I'd give you five bucks for lunch.' So, that's what I did. I stopped, at uh . . . on Flannery Road. . . ."

"That's your house, right?" Reese asked.
"Yeah."
"What's the address there?"
"2680 Flannery Road."
"What'd you do there?"
"Picked up some dirty clothes."
"Okay, earlier you said you picked up some dog food, too?"
"Yeah, I did pick up some dog food."
"Where did you pick the girl up at?" Breshears interrupted. "You said on an on ramp?"
"In Berkeley."
"Do you remember what on ramp, to what freeway?"
"To the 280 there," Singleton responded, referring to the 280 freeway.
"Do you know which on ramp it was?"
Singleton thought for a moment. "Yeah, it was at the foot of University Avenue."
"Okay. Thank you," Reese said politely.
It was standard cop technique. Make the subject comfortable. Keep him talking, all the way into prison.
"So, then I left and started to Sparks," Singleton continued.
He stubbed out his cigarette and lit up another, blew out some smoke, and smothered the match in an ashtray.
"The young lady told me she has a sister that lives in Reno. So I said, 'Well, we ought to be there in an hour and a half or so.' So I stopped for gas in Auburn. And she went to the restroom and I got the gas, then I went to the restroom. Came back, she got in the car."
"What kind of service station was that that you stopped at, do you remember?" Breshears wondered.
"It was an Exxon."
"Do you know what time that was about?"
"Oh, it was around five o'clock, five-thirty."
"P.M.? In the evening?"
"Yeah, P.M. So, the young lady come back and got in the van. Soon as I pull out of the station, she got a surveyor's stick from somewhere, I don't know where she got the goddamn thing, and tapped me upside

the head with it, and says, 'You're gonna drive me to L.A.' I said, 'Lady put the stick away. I'll take you anywhere you want to go.'"

"Where did she get the stick from? Was it in the van?" Breshears asked.

"I don't really know where it come from," Singleton answered. "But I don't recall having it in the van. Anyway, I told her, I said, 'Look, why don't I just take you back over here on this on ramp, nobody has to wait more than a couple minutes there and you'll get a ride within five minutes.' . . . So, then she tells me if I don't take her to L.A., she's going to stick me in the eyes and in the stomach. And I told her, I said, 'Lady just keep the stick down, and I'll take you anywhere you want to go.'"

"So, then she says that I'm bullshitting. I told her, 'I don't bullshit' I figured I had to. I had to take her to L.A. She said that unless I followed through, she told me she was going to say that I assaulted her. All right, so we drive down to . . . what's the name of that town? I think it's somewhere where I got the root beer. . . .'"

"Galt?" Breshears questioned him.

"Is Galt down that way?"

"Galt is south of Sacramento."

"Well, we drove down and stopped at the A & W."

"Do you remember what you had to eat?"

"I had a hot dog. It was hotter than hell. I got two big root beers."

"What did she have?"

"Truthfully, I don't recall. I think she had a sundae or something."

"Did you have to ask directions how to get to the A & W?"

"Yes, I did."

"Where did you ask your directions at?"

"I don't know. I think it was a business. So, at any rate, we get there, she takes the van keys. There was a huntin' knife in the van, which she picks up. . . . So I told her she could have anything she wanted to eat. She was a little bit belligerent and hollered. At any rate, she hadn't even eaten what she ordered."

Breshears didn't really care what Singleton or the girl had eaten. The idea was, if you could trap the suspect in an insignificant lie, such as what they had eaten or not eaten, he would eventually break down on the really key details and ultimately confess. It was a tactic that, time and again, worked during the police's questioning of suspects.

"So, then I wanted to get some cigarettes. I was out," Singleton continued, puffing on his cigarette. "I looked in the machine and they didn't have the brand that I smoked, so I drove over to another store and I got some 7-Up, and I think a bottle of milk."

"What kind of cigarettes do you smoke?"

"Pall Mall 100s."

"Is that Pall Mall Golds?"

"Yeah. So then, we start back on the freeway and there's two guys hitchhiking there and she says why don't I pick them up. So I stopped and picked them up."

"Where was this at on the freeway?"

"I don't recall but it was just before the on ramp on there."

"In Galt?"

"Yeah."

"What did they look like?"

"Well, one of them was almost my size and blond, sorta weather-beaten and he had a beard on him."

"How old would you say he was?

"I'd say he's about thirty-five."

"Do you recall what he was wearing?"

"Yeah, he was wearing [a] denim jacket, denim pants, and a sorta grayish sweater."

"What about the other guy?"

"The other guy was more Mexican descent, and he had quite an accent there, too."

"What did he look like?"

"Well, he was shorter. I guess about 5'6" and heavy, a little heavy set."

"How old a guy would you say he was?"

"It would be hard to guess, but I'd say somewhere between, anywhere from thirty to forty or maybe twenty-five, but I wouldn't say younger."

"What was he wearing?"

"Well, I don't know whether it was sort of a old military wool coat or a leather one. Well, it's wasn't military but it was sorta like a, you know, Eisenhower jacket."

Singleton was referring to the tight, body-hugging jacket that Eisenhower had made popular during World War II.

"What color was it?"

"A faded brown."

"What else did he have on?"

"A sweater and also I think he had sort of heavy gray pants on. They were heavy."

"Were the two guys together?"

Singleton answered, "Oh yeah, they were together," nodding vigorously.

"Did they seem like they knew each other?"

"Yeah, they knew each other well, because now, as soon as they get in, the girl starts off and she asks did they have anything to smoke or to blast. So then, I forgot which one of them broke out a 'reefer,' and she told them that I was giving her a bad time, you know, a rough time. But then I told them, I said, 'Look fellas, I'm just out having fun and I'm not giving anybody a bad time. The lady said she wants to go to L.A. She wants to go to L.A., we'll go to L.A.'"

"Where were they going?"

"San Bernardino," Singleton answered promptly. "That's what they told me. So, then the girl said she wanted to get stoned. So I said, 'Well, honey, if you want to get stoned, I got plenty of money.' And, so the guy who called himself Larry I think it was, what did I say his last name was?"

"I don't think you ever gave me a last name," said Reese. "Larry is one guy and the other is . . ." Reese looked at Singleton expectantly.

"Pedro."

"Right, Pedro"

"It was Larry Schmidt. And through the conversation there he said that he'd been in the marines and he had a bad discharge. About this time I'm really beginning to worry about myself see . . ."

"Up until this time, had you had anything to drink?"

"I'd had two drinks in Berkeley and one drink after . . . I had one drink sitting there then. . . . I put alcohol in a drink . . . and that son of a bitch spilled it. That's right, I remember—"

Breshears interrupted. "You put alcohol in a drink? Where was this at?"

"I put a drink in that root beer and then that spilled."

"Did you have anything to drink from your house down to A & W? Did you have any liquor with you?" Breshears continued.

"Yes, I did."

"What did you have with you?"

"I had vodka and mixed with straight alcohol."

Straight alcohol is 200 proof.

"How big a bottle of vodka did you have?"

"What I did, I poured two quarts and one quart . . . a quart of water in a gallon."

"In a gallon bottle?"

"Yeah."

"So you had a one gallon bottle with you?"

"Yes.

That was one part of his story Breshears didn't doubt. Merchant marines were notorious for their consumption of booze. They liked to mix 200-proof alcohol and cut it with water, in exactly the way Singleton was describing.

"So, then that drink was spilled, yeah, that's right," Singleton continued. "Well, I think, I might as well have another drink, see, so I poured myself another. So then the girl says she's drinking. She asked this Larry could he drive. He said yeah. I said, 'If you want to drive, you can drive.' We stopped and he started driving then."

"Why did you want Larry to drive?" Breshears wondered.

"I didn't want him to drive, I just didn't want to get in no goddamn argument and with a knife on top of me."

"Who had a knife on top of you?" Breshears asked sharply.

"Well, the girl still had the knife."

Singleton was on a roll; they let their suspect continue.

"Yeah, I got out two times, I remember that. But she had the knife in her hand and my car keys. So, okay, she mentioned she wanted to stay stoned so I told the guys, 'I got plenty of money. If you want anything, we'll stop and get it.' Then they went down, I don't know how many miles down there, but turned off the road and went back over there to the east over to some highway and come back towards the north. I know we come back to the north. We stopped at some tavern. I didn't really pay much attention. And Larry goes on and then about two minutes later, this old green pickup truck, it still had the old California plates on it. So the guys, they get out and they dicker awhile and they get a package, two packages, I don't know nothing 'bout dope, see, I was just bluffing."

"You don't remember what tavern this is?"

"No, I don't even know what town it was. I don't even know how far south down there it was. But, at any rate, they get back in and they're sniffing, like they done cocaine and they're stoned by that time."

"Where did they get the stuff that they sniffed?"

"They bought it from this guy in the black pickup."

Now it was black. A couple of minutes before, the pickup was green.

"It was fairly good-sized parking lot there on both sides. I wasn't paying too much goddamn attention, like uh, I was playing the game room. Now all three are having a drink and they are sniffing... and so then Christ, we drive up and park."

"You said all three of them had a drink. You weren't drinking?" Breshears asked.

"Yeah, I was drinking," Singleton admitted.

"Which one wasn't drinking?"

"All three of them was drinking."

"There was four of you," Breshears reminded him amiably.

"Well, I mean..." Singleton stumbled.

"All of you?"

"Yeah."

"Did you sniff any of the stuff?"

"No I didn't sniff it, no. I pretended to. I don't know anything about that shit. But, okay, now everybody's happy so we stop and I think there was a light there."

"Just right by the freeway?"

Singleton shook his head.

"No, this was still on that old highway. And so, we got to kidding around there and by that time now I know, this is going to sound bad, too, but for twenty years I had this old .22 short pistol. Lot of times I go out planking [shooting] with it."

"You mean in Nevada?"

"In Nevada. This time I didn't even know the goddamn thing was in the car. Okay, now Pedro tells the girl, 'Well now you don't need the knife. I have the pistol.'"

"Where did he find the pistol at?"

"I'll be goddamned if I know."

"You don't know where you put it in your own van?" Breshears did nothing to disguise the incredulity in his voice.

"I don't know. Maybe it was in the glove compartment. Normally I hide the thing under the carpet down the driver's side. So, okay, so now everybody's pretty goddamn drunk. These guys are talking about money. He suddenly remembered something. "What I didn't say was the last place we stopped at, I had taken my money and put it in my sock in about three different places and stuck my wallet up over the sun visor."

"Where were they sitting?"

"They were on the toolbox."

"Were you in the back of the van or were you in the . . ."

"I was in the seat."

"Passenger seat?"

"Yeah."

"And Larry was driving?"

"Yeah. So, I was halfway kidding, when I told the girl, 'How much would you charge to make love to everybody?' And she was laughing and I think I give her eighty bucks, approximately eighty dollars, something like that. So then she said she liked to suck cocks, so okay, she gives Larry a blow job. I could've actually cared less, so what I done was trying to keep on one side so I could get out of the van. So, Christ I laid down, I got in the back and I laid down and she give me a blow job. So then she refused to give Pedro one. I don't remember all the goddamn details, but at any rate, she turned around and sat on top of me."

"Did she take her clothes off?"

"Yes, she took her clothes off."

"Did you take yours off?"

"I, uh, took my pants down."

"What kind of pants were you wearing?"

"Oh, a blue border suit."

"You were wearing a suit?" asked Breshears, barely hiding the surprise in his voice.

"Yeah," he answered, a little defensively.

Reese eyed the tape recorder and noticed that the takeup reel was almost full.

"Okay," said Reese, "we're getting pretty close to the end of this tape, so I'll stop here and start another one. The time will be 19:54 hours."

FOUR

The Golden Gate Bridge sparkled in the fall sunshine. Cars slipped across her span effortlessly, while below, fishing boats chugged back into the harbor with all kinds of fish that would wind up in the stalls at Fisherman's Wharf.

Sal Benedetto had decided to go fishing that morning. He usually got there early, but that morning, he had some extra chores to do around the house and did not arrive at the shoreline until just before noon. Still, it was a weekday and no one was around. Most fishermen preferred going to sea and the few that fished off the rocks, tended to do so a little bit farther down the coastline, where the water wasn't as polluted. That meant that most mornings, Sal had his favorite shoreline under the bridge all to himself.

He reached back and cast his line in and after it played out, set the reel on drag. If a fish bit, it'd get some line and then he'd pull and snag the hook in its mouth. That was the plan, until he happened to look off to his right. That's when he saw what looked like a human hand. He gazed at it a while, focusing, trying to figure out if his eyes were playing tricks in the hot sun. When he realized that they were not, he wedged his pole into a rock and walked toward the object.

When he was but a few feet away, he got a good look at it. He was right. It was a hand. How did it get there? Sal wondered. He didn't speculate long. Better to call the cops and let them take care of it.

Sal Benedetto went to get the cops, leaving one of Mary Vincent's severed hands on the rock behind him.

While Reese changed reels, Breshears stepped outside to think.

For the most part, Breshears knew that Singleton was lying. There had been no evidence that Singleton had picked up any male hitchhikers. The girl had been very explicit: it was Singleton, and no one else, in his van.

What he was telling the truth about was the drinking. One look at his red-veined nose told the story—this was a hard drinker, probably an alcoholic. The real question was when he got drunk, did he black out and keep going? If he did, he could have no memory of any assault, or at least claim he didn't. That would allow his attorney, when he did get one, to introduce a diminished capacity defense.

The fact was that the law said that if a person was drunk and committed a homicide, he wasn't fully capable of understanding his actions and therefore not as culpable. That was crazy, but the law was the law, no two ways about it.

The best thing Breshears could do here was to give Singleton enough rope to hang himself. Keep him talking, trap him in lies, and then maybe get him to make an admission, some sort of statement that could be used against him at trial.

"You were telling me what you were wearing that night," Breshears began after the break.

"Like I said, I was wearing a blue border suit," said Singleton with exasperation.

"Blue border suit. Is that a two-piece suit?"

"The same as this thing here," Singleton answered, pointing to what he had on. Breshears looked him over.

"So, like coveralls, that's what you were wearing, like now?"

"Yeah, like coveralls," Singleton agreed.

"Okay, and when did you say you took them off?"

"No, I just pulled them down was all I did."

"Hold up there just one second. Didn't you say that she sat on top of you?"

"Yeah, she sat on top of me . . . down there."

It would almost be amusing. The alleged rapist mutilator was embarrassed to use the word "penis."

"Did Larry take his clothes off?"

"He took his pants off, yeah, and his jacket."

"Did she say why she didn't want anything to do with Pedro?"

"Said something about how he was a 'fat Mexican.'"

"Okay."

"That was original. Singleton was trying to characterize the victim as a racist.

"She said she wanted to stay stoned all the time. So then I tell these guys," Singleton continued, "I said 'Why worry about L.A?' I put my paycheck down and said, 'I got plenty of these. I get a couple of them a week.' And I had a check there for about $800 and I don't think they could read too good. I said, 'Look at this, I got two more of them.' I tell them, 'Let's knock this off and we'll go back to San Francisco and I'll cash the checks and we'll all have plenty of money to stay stoned for a week. These guys said, 'Well, we could do a little business.'"

"What kind of business?"

"I guess dope business. So Christ, that's when Pedro tried to drive the goddamn van."

"When you guys were putting the make to the girl, was the van stopped or was it moving?"

"It was stopped and moving. Larry—"

"What do you mean?" Breshears cut in

"Larry was putting the make to her while Pedro almost run into the ditch."

"Who was driving when you put the make to her?"

"It was stopped then."

"Do you recall where you were at?"

"No. I'd never been in that part of the country down there before."

"Was it by the freeway, or stopped on the side of a freeway?"

"No, it was off on a blacktop road down there somewhere."

"Straight road, flat road?"

"Yeah it was straight road and flat top and, uh . . . oh yeah, I didn't fuck there though. We stopped and went over to this shack. And, oh shit, by this time it was getting around ten and I'll tell ya the goddamn truth, they said they was going to break into the shack and get something."

"What were they going to get?"

"I'll be goddamn if I can remember. But there was an old shack there, but Christ by this time I was wondering what the hell was they going to do."

"Was there a reason why you don't remember?"

"I don't really remember what they was going to do," Singleton answered in a low, almost inaudible voice.

"What happened then?"

"Well, I could hear this door being forced open, and I said 'Oh shit.' See, I did this one time before. I picked up some hitchhikers halfway up here and they had booze with them and I went to sleep in the van and woke up in front of a bar. They were all teenagers and I took a rap there for contributing and I didn't have a damn thing to do with it."

"What happened this time, Larry?"

"Well, to tell you the goddamn truth about it, oh shit, Pedro started to drive again and Larry and her was sitting on the floor. She's nude and Christ I just . . . to tell you the truth I passed out. Now, when I come to again, we were on the goddamn freeway. And, if I remember, shit, we're almost where the highway splits."

"Where's that at?"

"Where 5 splits to San Francisco. I don't know what the number is there."

"Uh-huh. Who was driving?"

"The Mexican, and he was going about seventy-five and a little bit erratic so I calmed him down and told him, I said, 'Look, hey, let's let me drive because if we screw up here we'll end up in jail.'"

"Where was Larry?"

"He was sitting in the other seat."

"Where was the girl?"

"The girl wasn't there at the time."

"Uh-huh."

"So I get up, he stops, and I asked him, I said, 'Where's our pigeon at?' He says, 'Oh, she's already got her hands in the till. She's no good. We sent her to L.A.' That's the reason I didn't think a goddamn thing more about it. I figure, well . . ."

"What did you think about her clothes still being in the van?"

"Her clothes?" He sounded surprised. "I don't even . . . they weren't in the van . . . I . . . don't . . . even . . . know . . . know. . . . They weren't in the van, no, no, because them guys only took their stuff out of the van when I dropped them off."

"Where did you drop them off at?"

"At, uh, in San Francisco."

"You went into San Francisco?"

"Yeah, because, see, I showed them the address where the union hall is there and I told them that's where I work and I get plenty of money and the bank's right around there. So I give them the rest of my money and by then, I had forty dollars. I told them, 'You guys get a clock and I'll meet you right back here at ten in the morning when the bank opens.'"

"Do you remember where you dropped them off at in San Francisco?"

"Yeah, at Sixth and Mission. Right on skid row."

"What did you do from there, after they were gone?"

"I turned right around and went back down to Fifth and over the freeway and got some sleep and—"

"Where was this at?"

"Huh?"

"Where did you go to get some sleep?"

"Over at my Flannery residence."

"That's your house?"

"Yeah, and I figured, well, that's a goddamn two-hundred-dollar lesson."

"Okay," Reese cut in, "earlier in the day, we obtained some consent to searches from you. Remember that? One for your van that's a '70—"

"'71'" Singleton corrected him.

"Blue Ford van," Reese continued. "Also for the house at 826—"

"Glenbrook."

"Glenbrook, that's your place right?"

"That's right," Singleton nodded.

"Also, you gave me a consent to search for a blue toolbox which you had taken out of the van and put in the garage?"

"Yeah."

"Also a consent to search for a '78 T-bird that belongs to you?"

"Yes."

"Okay, now the consent to search for the T-bird was because of the fact that you said the coveralls you were wearing, blue in color with a zipper front..."

"Yeah."

"Were in the trunk."

"I said they *might* be in the trunk, didn't I? Did I say they *were* in the trunk?"

"You said they were in the trunk," Reese confirmed. "You put them in there after you washed them."

"Well, obviously I made a mistake, 'cause, see, I kind of thought they should be ... should be three jumpsuits in there ... a green one—"

"Okay, mainly we were interested in the blue—"

"And two blue ones," Singleton continued.

"There was a blue toolbox," Reese added, "and we asked for a consent to search for that because you said that you had owned a hatchet."

"A small hatchet," Breshears added, smiling easily.

"Yeah, so?

"And that you believed that hatchet was in the toolbox. Is that correct?" Reese asked.

"Yeah."

Breshears noticed it then, a thin sheen of perspiration forming on Singleton's forehead.

"Now there's some inconsistencies from what I recall earlier today and what you're saying now," Reese went on. "Earlier today you said that you gave Larry fifty dollars to purchase that dope."

"Yeah, I said approximately that."

"Did you give him the money or did he have the money?"

42

"I give him the money."

"Also, you said when you woke up, Larry was driving the van in San Francisco. Was it Larry driving or the other guy driving?"

"The other guy."

"Okay, earlier today, I asked if you ever remembered the girl being tied up. Do you remember what you said to that?"

"I said no, I never remember seeing her tied up."

"Also, earlier today, I asked if there would be any reason for there being blood on your coveralls. Do you remember that?"

"Yes, you did."

"First you told me no. Then later you told me something about a bloody nose."

"Yeah, I said that they were horsing around and then actually I can get bloody any time off here in small amounts. The lady that rents the house from me, she washed that stuff for me and no, I mean I don't think it was. Also you can ask Hank over there, because Hank helped me clean out the van."

His rambling was almost incoherent. It was time to steer him back on track.

"You mentioned something about her having a bloody nose," Breshears reminded him.

"I can vaguely recall something like that, driving along and she fell over and hit Pedro's elbow or something like that. I just don't know."

"Did it cause her nose to bleed?"

"I don't really remember if it did or not."

"When did you leave your home in San Pablo? After you went back to bed and got up? What time did you leave to go to Sparks?"

"Around ten A.M. I guess."

"Did you do anything around the house in San Pablo before you left? Clean up or anything?"

"No, never did."

"Did you start a fire in the fireplace?"

"Oh yeah, I burned up the paper."

"Did you burn anything besides paper?"

"Uh. Yeah, I burned several old rags I had there."

"Several old rags?"

"Yeah, see, in my work there I come home with bags full of rags and before I left there I did burn 'em."

"Why did you burn the rags? Why didn't you just keep those and wash those, too?"

"Because it's a needless expense to me."

"What color are those rags?"

"All different colors I guess."

"What colors are there? Do you get them at work?"

"Yeah."

"Okay, what colors are they?"

"Uh, there's every color."

"What colors do you remember?"

"There's blue, white . . ."

"All the same material?"

"No."

"They're not all the same material?"

"No."

"Are they supplied by a linen shop?"

"Uh, uh, what you do is order a hundred-pound bundle of rags."

"Who do you order them from?"

"From Chip's Ship Handlers."

"They're all pretty much the same brand then?"

"Well, I'll tell you the damn truth, I don't know where they buy them. I guess there's a half dozen different suppliers."

"Do you remember picking up the clothes from your house?"

"Yeah."

Reese cut in. "Do you recall what was in them, the clothes you brought to Sparks?"

"Well, there was, uh . . . underwear and shorts for about two weeks and, uh . . ."

"Any female clothes in there?"

"No, there was no female clothes in there."

"None at all?" Breshears shot back. Singleton's head was spinning like a top.

"No!" he shouted.

"Any of your daughter's clothes?" Breshears kept on.

"Yeah, there was one white . . . white . . . white, uh, blouse that she left."

"How did the panties and bras get in there?"

Singleton looked up at Breshears.

"In where?"

"In your dirty clothes."

"Oh, that uh . . . that was a bunch that I was going to give . . . you see my ex-wife passed away down there and her clothes was still in the house and—"

Breshears cut in. "These bras were for a small person. They wouldn't fit your deceased wife." This time he did nothing to hide the sarcasm in his voice.

"Oh, then they're my daughter's. My daughter just throws her stuff over there."

Breshears looked down at the sheet in front of him. Someone had already interviewed Singleton's daughter. Then he looked up.

"But she hasn't been there since the beginning of summer."

"She's over there every day."

"She hasn't been at the house in San Pablo since the beginning of the summer though. How would her clothes get mixed in with your dirty clothes?"

"Because . . ."

"I talked to your daughter, and she has her clothes down where she's staying at," said Breshears.

"I know that but, . . . well see, my daughter is a typical teenager, she leaves everything around."

"But she doesn't live over at that house, and across the street from where she lives there's someone does her laundry. Surely she doesn't wander around and leave her bras lying around? Take them off and leave them in with your dirty clothes?"

"Well, now . . . uh . . . there's a whole bunch of her, uh . . . last year's pants, trousers, and whatnot there in the garage. You can ask her."

"I did. I just talked to her."

"This hatchet that you have," Reese cut in, "can you describe it to us?"

"Yes. Uh . . . it's just a regular red small hatchet, about a fourteen-inch handle on it."

"What color is it?"

"I believe it's red."

"Wood handle?" Reese asked.

"Yeah, wood handle."

"Got anything tied to it or anything?"

"Yeah it's got a little . . ."

"Little piece of rope?"

"Little piece of rope, yeah."

"What do you use that hatchet for?"

"Well, I don't use it, part of the year only. See, like that other gear in that box there is for pulling some car out of the ditch, or else if I get that van stuck I can pull it a hundred foot."

"I notice that the little rope in there had been cut," said Breshears. "Any reason why it was cut?"

"Uh . . . there's a reason why it was cut . . ."

"What was that?"

"I was moving furniture with it."

"And you cut it? Apparently, looking at it, it's been cut with a knife. Not too sharp of a knife at that."

"Well let's see what the devil did I . . .? Had to tie something with it and pull . . . but really hard to tackle, uh? Well, I moved furniture in that van quite a bit, and then use it to tie the furniture with."

"You're a seaman. You don't cut the knots. You tie them. You wouldn't cut them with a knife, would you?"

"Yeah. I cut it because . . . because you notice that, uh, most of that can be respliced right back in it."

"It was cut in two places, though."

"I don't know."

The sweat was pouring off Singleton now. Breshears saw it and moved in.

"Mr. Singleton, I've talked to this girl several times . . ."

"Yeah."

"And she's told us what happened. She was awake when you cut her arms off."

"Well, I'll tell you . . ."

"She remembers you."

"Now . . . no . . . that . . . I don't have enough guts to cut anybody's arm off and I don't . . . I'll swear on the Bible I did not cut that girl's arms off."

"And then you walked, rather you put her down, you kicked her into a pipe right down there in the dirt."

"I did not, sir."

"She was awake when you did this."

"I did not, sir."

"You took her out of the van . . ."

"Nah . . ."

"You laid her down after taking the rope off. . . ." "Nah . . . Nah . . ."

"And you chopped her arms off one at a time."

"That's an absolute lie. I did not."

"Then why would she say it was somebody else when she knows it's you? She drew your picture."

"Well . . . there was that . . ."

"Nobody else in the van, just you and her."

"No, no, that's an absolute lie, too!"

"Why did you wash and clean the van the day you got back? You washed your jumpsuit, you washed the van, you washed the rug inside the van, but you didn't wash the dirty clothes that you picked up."

"The dirty clothes that I picked up, uh . . . were washed. . . . Trudy washed all the dirty clothes I picked up. That bunch of clothes that you're looking at there in the garage there belongs to my daughter and my ex-wife, which I was going to . . . to . . . send to Goodwill up here."

"Why did you clean the van when you got back? You took the rug out, washed it. . . ."

"Because the goddamn thing . . . like I say there was several drinks spilled on it . . . and, uh . . . here it was there was half a dozen drinks spilled on that thing and then normally down there the water is higher and I always routinely wash the van or the car when the water is up. See, there's a water shortage and the water is high down there, and so it's a normal, routine thing for me to do, to take and cut off that . . . Now that's the first time that, uh . . . I've washed that carpet out though. I mean you can ask . . . it was wet as hell all over and . . . and . . . several . . . it . . ."

"Do you remember earlier today when I said that if someone else was in that van, any other people, that should be able to develop some kind of fingerprints and you said no because you washed the whole inside of that van out?" said Reese.

"Yeah, I think I washed it out. . . . Yeah . . . absolutely . . . I washed the windows in that damn thing."

"Would there be any reason for there being blood on that hatchet of yours?"

"No, I . . ."

Reese looked down at the tape recorder; the spindle was almost empty.

"Okay, this will be the end of this tape. 20:22 hours."

The two cops had Singleton where they wanted him. He was now on the run, denying any involvement with Mary Vincent's mutilation, concocting some cock-and-bull story about two other hitchhikers being responsible. And while Breshears and Reese knew they would have to check out his story on the outside chance he was telling the truth they were really hoping that, as they entered the last round of questioning, they could elicit a confession. Because, if they could do that, they could clear the case and get back to more mundane felonies, not to mention avoiding a lengthy and expensive trial.

FIVE

Murphy and Puell were the two cops who responded to Sal Benedetto's sighting of the severed hand on the rocks of San Francisco Bay. When they arrived, they couldn't believe their luck.

It *had* to be Mary Vincent's hand, it just *had* to be. How many other severed hands' cases did they have that needed to be cleared?

The hand was packed in ice in an Igloo cooler, and transported back to headquarters, where detectives took charge. They put in a call to Modesto to tell them of their find. Then, they brought it to the coroner's office, where Roland Prahl, chief deputy coroner for the Alameda County sheriff's department, took over, and began his examination.

He noticed that the epidermal or outer layer of the skin was completely washed away. That would be consistent with the amount of time since the assault, which was approaching ten days. Despite the skin's decomposition, there was a patch of reddish-brown nail polish that remained on the tip of the nail of the right thumb. Had Mary Vincent been wearing red nail polish?

The phone lines heated up between the San Francisco and Modesto police and the answer arrived soon enough: Mary had, indeed, painted her nails red prior to the mutilation. To facilitate comparison, doctors in Modesto sent fragments of bone taken from Mary during surgery to Oakland, where Prahl compared it to the bone of the hand.

The comparison was positive. X rays of the severed bones in Mary's forearm also matched the severed bones in the hand's wrist.

How large was San Francisco Bay? What were the odds that a hand thrown in one of its estuaries upriver would eventually tumble down into the bay, let alone wash up relatively intact on a rock? Prahl later told the press that matching the hand fished out of the drink to Mary beat "astronomical odds, far more than the proverbial needle in a haystack." And that was true.

What had made the find possible was the natural gas that builds up in decomposing human tissue. The gas had kept the hand afloat, allowing it to sail along undisturbed like a piece of driftwood. Had that bloating not occurred and had it sunk to the bottom of the bay, scavenger fish would have dined on it and the evidence would literally have been eaten up.

But now, they had the hand, and they had a match.

"There is no question at all," Prahl stated, that the two matched.

What was unclear was how long the limb had been in the water, or for that matter, how long her assailant had carried it around with him before he threw it in the drink. No matter.

When he came to trial, it would be used against him.

"This will be side 3. Time starting 20:22 hours. Okay, do you remember the last question?" Reese began.

"Why was there blood on the hatchet?" Singleton asked reasonably.

"Would there be any reason for any blood being on the hatchet?" Reese corrected him.

"No, not to my knowledge. There shouldn't be any blood on it. Although . . . I . . . never even went hunting this year, so . . ."

"Do you remember earlier today that I told you that I don't see any reason for this young lady to be lying if there was two other people in that van, she should have said there was two other people in that van?"

"Well, I don't know why she's lying either, but like all I know is I'm telling you the story just the way that it happened."

"Well, you said yourself you didn't remember because you thought you were passed out, or at least you didn't remember," Breshears pointed out.

"Now wait just a minute," Singleton protested. "I don't remember the girl getting out of the van."

"Why do you think that this girl would lie about somebody else cutting her arms off when she was conscious the entire time it was happening?" asked Breshears.

"Sir, I—"

"Why do you think she would say you did it if somebody else chopped her arms off?"

"I don't have the slightest idea, but I cannot . . . I could never raise a weapon to anybody. . . ."

"She said at one time you threatened to blow her head off with a shotgun when you'd been drinking. She says you get extremely violent when you've been drinking," Reese said.

"How about last summer when you beat your daughter?" Breshears chimed in.

"I didn't beat my daughter! I spanked my daughter's bottom. She called me a liar!"

Which is what you are, Breshears thought. Instead, he said, "How about when she had to go to the hospital and have her face treated because you hit her with your fist?"

"I didn't hit her with my fist," Singleton protested in a hurt tone.

"It's on record in the hospital," Breshears stated matter-of-factly.

"That girl is . . . now wait just a minute. You can ask the people where she stayed at. They found out and they know all about that. I told them the truth."

"They told *me* also."

"Now my daughter's strong as an ox. She was . . . and I didn't know my daughter was that strong, now . . . Like I'd been working about nineteen hours and I had about three or four drinks. I come home and she stands there and calls me a fat liar. I tell her, I says, 'Dammit, if you call me a liar again, I'm going to spank your bottom.'"

"Were you in the military?"

"Yes, I was."

"In Korea?" Reese asked, knowing the answer because he'd already pulled Singleton's war record.

"Yes."

"In combat?" Reese pressed.

"Yes."

"And you were worried about a girl you say was holding a stick on you in the van? Come on."

"Well, there's a lot of difference. . . ." Singleton hedged.

"She readily admits she held a stick on you," said Breshears.

"I beg your pardon?"

"She readily admits she held a stick on you," the cop repeated.

"She hit me with the goddamn thing," Singleton suddenly remembered.

"Remember earlier today I asked you if you'd read anything or if you knew anything about this story? You know about the young lady out here with her arms chopped off and being sexually assaulted, and you told me, 'No,' that you hadn't been reading the newspaper? You hadn't?" Reese asked.

"I told you that I had not followed the story at all."

"Okay."

"No . . . uh . . . I think I saw it on TV . . . but to tell you the damn truth about it . . . I never even . . . never even give it a thought. . . ."

"Your daughter says that during the time you stayed in Sparks, after coming over from here, you were acting strange and drinking rather heavily, emotionally upset. Seems like you're concerned about something."

"Yeah, I am concerned that my goddamn knee is swelled up again on me, and the doctor tells me I might have cancer in my throat, and I'll tell you the damn truth about it, my ex-wife went down with cancer and I don't want to face cancer."

"Did you also take an overdose of pills?" Breshears asked.

"No, I didn't take an overdose."

"Did you end up in the hospital where they treated you for an overdose with pills and liquor combination?"

After a pause, Singleton answered with a quiet "Yes." He was ashamed that he had tried to kill himself.

"Did you take all those pills? Seconal pills?"

"No, hell no!"

"Why did your roommate have to come through the window to get in your room?"

"Well, I locked the bedroom door. Those doors, the dog opens them. We got that dog there and all he does is jump up and open the doors. That's the reason I locked the door."

Reese asked, "Can you explain to me then why this girl, who has nothing to lose at all whatsoever by telling us that there was somebody else in that van, can recall everything? And you tell us the same story, except you say there were two other people in that van?"

"I can't explain nothing to you. All I know is that there was a lot of . . . everyone being blasted . . . sniffing in that van, and also, there was a lot of booze in that van."

"Mr. Singleton," Breshears asked respectfully, "what did she do to anger you?"

"She didn't do . . . actually, she didn't . . . truthfully . . . I told you that . . . I told her just to take it easy. . . ."

"Did she take it easy?"

"Yeah, in a way, but by that time she's got the goddamn knife and won't let me have the car keys. Okay, then she starts, uh . . . playing one against the other and then she asked them did they . . . oh, I forgot what she said about . . ."

"Mr. Singleton we know what happened," Breshears said gently. "You readily admit that you picked her up, and we know the outcome of it and perhaps I can understand why."

"Well now . . ."

"There's got to be a reason," Reese said, as much to himself as to Singleton.

"There's a reason," Breshears answered. "What is the reason, Mr. Singleton?"

"Why?" Reese wondered.

"There has to be a reason," Breshears insisted.

Singleton looked frantically from one man to the other. "I'm telling you the God's truth," Singleton said, imploringly. "You gotta believe me—I don't know anything more. Now I brought those guys back to

San Francisco and I was shook up myself. I was worried about my life at the time."

"Why were you worried about your life?" Breshears asked. "You didn't know what happened to her?"

"I swear to God I didn't even know the girl met with foul play."

"Then why were you worried about your life?"

"Christ, there's a gun and a knife in there, I got three strangers in the car. . . ."

"What did you think about this story when you read it in the paper and saw it on television?" Reese asked.

"I'll tell you the goddamn truth, I . . . I . . . didn't even give it a second thought, really."

"Mr. Singleton, what did she do to upset you or to get you angry or get you in a fit of rage?" Breshears persisted.

"She didn't get me in a fit of rage," he answered defensively.

"Mr. Singleton, isn't it really that she knew too much about you and you got scared?"

"No, sir, definitely not."

"Then why did you tie her hands up behind her back?"

"I did not tie her up . . . that girl was . . ."

"Mr. Singleton, we served a search warrant on your house in San Pablo. We've got the material out of that fireplace."

"What material is that?" Singleton asked innocently.

"The majority of the burned ashes and the cloth material."

"All you got is a bunch of rags there."

"That will be tested and we're gonna know for sure. We'll know *positively*."

"All right, but all there are is a bunch of rags there."

"There's blood on that hatchet," Reese reminded him.

There was no such thing. The hatchet had not been recovered. But if they could get Singleton to admit that he used it to cut the girl's arms off, maybe he'd give them a confession. Lord knew they were working hard enough to get it.

"Well, if there's blood on that hatchet, I don't know anything about it, because I sure as hell didn't use it."

"This young lady picked you out of a photo lineup and is saying that you're the man that did it. She says that you're the man that chopped her arms off."

"Now what did I do to make her mad is what I'm trying to figure out?" Singleton asked, scratching his head.

"She wasn't mad. She was in pain. She was barely conscious. She described you and continued to describe you all the way along. All the way through," said Breshears.

"But..."

"And as she got a little better, she described you more and more and more. And she's the one that directed that composite of you."

"Well, I'll tell you God's truth about it, I don't know what she—"

"Don't blame her."

"Because... I..."

"Don't give me the God's truth unless you're going to tell me the whole truth, Mr. Singleton," Breshears continued.

"I'm telling you the whole truth, sir."

"You're the one that's going to have to live with it on your conscience."

"Well, I'll tell you—"

"And it's obvious that you're doing a poor job of it right now. Are you going to continue to be able to live like this, with this inside you, not letting it come out?"

"I'm letting... I'm letting everything I know come out."

"The biggest concern that she wants to know right now is what happened to her hands after they were removed with the ax. She knows. She watched you. She watched you chop them off."

"I did not chop anybody's—"

"She could—"

"I could not.... I could not..."

"Maybe you couldn't—"

"... pull a weapon on anybody that...."

"Maybe you couldn't, but you did."

"No, sir, I did not."

"She saw you do it. Three chops on the left arm. Five chops on the right arm. Then you threw her— in that gully.... You kicked her into that pipe..."

"She's lying!"

"She got up and walked out, Mr. Singleton, and you didn't know she'd survived."

"She's lying!"

"You didn' t know she walked out. You left her there to die. You took those hands off to cover up a crime."

"I did not, sir."

"You didn't want anybody to identity her because she got up and walked out. And when she walked out, she identified you. She even said she feels sorry for you, Mr. Singleton. She really feels sorry for you now."

"Well, I'll tell you guys the truth about it. I don't know what I did to make her mad, and—"

"I know what you did," Breshears answered. "You cut her arms off, that's what you did."

"I could not use a weapon on anybody."

"Why did you tell your ex-wife you were going to blow her to hell with a shotgun?" Reese interrupted him.

"Oh Christ, I don't even own a shotgun."

"Mr. Singleton, what did you do with her hands?" Breshears asked.

"Sir, I had . . . I don't even know where the girl went to, that's the reason I did not even realize what went on. I swear it!"

"Are you going to be able to live with this? Are you going to be able to live with this without telling somebody? Are you going to be able to look at her face-to-face and say, 'I didn't chop your arms off?"

"Well, I can look her right back and say that I did not do it, because something is definitely wrong there. Yes, sir, I will be able to do that."

"And she's going to look at you and she's going to tell you, 'You're the one who chopped my arms off.'"

"Well, I can look her right back and say that I did not do it, because something is definitely wrong there."

"That's right, something is wrong and we want to know *why*."

"Yeah?"

"There's got to be a reason, Mr. Singleton, why you did that."

"Could I get some more coffee? I did not chop that woman's arms off. I got a terrible temper, I admit that. I don't mind fighting, see, but insofar as using a weapon, no, I won't. I wouldn't even go hunting hardly anymore."

"What was it, Mr. Singleton, a last-minute thought to chop her arms off after you laid her down on the road?"

"I never..."

"Were you scared at the time?"

"I did not..."

"I would be scared at the time, Mr. Singleton. And I'd be scared right now, too."

"I—"

"And I don't think I could live with myself without telling somebody."

"I'm not scared because... like I told you the whole truth now and I'm gonna swear that's all I know."

"You're talking about a half a dozen drinks—not counting the ones that you spilled. You said yourself that when you sniffed that stuff that you didn't know what it was. You also told us that you didn't smoke marijuana."

"I didn't... I told... I... told you I don't smoke marijuana."

"Oh, then you were saying that you were blacked out during this period of time? First you woke up and you said Larry was driving, and then you said later that Pedro was driving."

"They both was driving."

"And that she didn't like him because he was a fat Mexican."

"That's... yeah, that's right... that's exactly what she told me."

"Then why doesn't she say there were two other guys in the car?"

"Sir, I don't know."

"Because there weren't two other guys in the car," Reese explained.

"Only one," Breshears added.

"You," Reese finished.

"There was two other guys in the car," Singleton continued to insist, "and I took them right back into San Francisco."

"You know it would seem to me, Mr. Singleton, that if she had herself a stick and you were that afraid of her—"

"Sir, it's not a matter of being afraid. I wouldn't... I don't want to hurt the girl."

"Well, then why did you hurt her? That's the reason we're here."

"*I did not hurt the girl.* To my knowledge, no. She told me that she was twenty or twenty-one and had been hooking. And I told her to get off the greasy kid stuff. I said, 'Hey, go for that. Go for one hundred dollars a day.'"

"When did you tell her this?"

"Sometime along there, I don't know. . . ."

"Uh-huh."

"And the other with it, see, but, uh . . ."

"Oh, this was after you picked them up when she told you that she was a prostitute. Is that what she said?"

"Yeah."

"What words did she use? What words did she say?"

"Well, she said she liked to suck cocks."

"So, automatically you assumed, 'Well, she must be a prostitute.'"

"I didn't assume, I . . ."

"Well, you were just saying you thought she was a prostitute."

"Well . . ."

"And you'd given her a hundred bucks."

"That's what I told her. 'Well hell, come along with me to get a hundred bucks a night.'"

"Did you give her money?" Reese asked.

"Yeah, I gave it to her. About eighty dollars."

"Okay, when you gave her this eighty dollars, did she refuse to do anything then?"

"No, she didn't refuse to do anything. She took her goddamn clothes off."

"Just tore the blouse right off, huh?" Breshears asked sarcastically.

"No, she didn't tear the blouse off."

"How did she take it off?"

"I'll be damned to hell if I know. How does a girl take her clothes off?"

"Well, I don't know. When your hands are tied behind your back, it's pretty difficult," Breshears shot back. "You told her, 'You'll be all right if you do exactly as I say.'"

"That's a lie! That's an absolute lie!"

"It's the truth!"

"No, sir." And Singleton violently shook his head.

"Why don't you tell us the truth?"

"I'm telling you the truth," Singleton pleaded.

"You told us the truth to the A & W station. Why don't you tell us the *rest* of the truth?"

"I am."

"Help yourself, Mr. Singleton," Breshears said sympathetically.

"Because . . . I . . . I can't tell you anything different but what actually went on."

"The girl told us exactly what happened."

"So am I!"

"Well, you stopped short and changed the story. She told the truth. She had nothing to hide. Her arms are gone. They're never going to be put back on. She wants to know what happened to them."

"I don't know . . ."

"Did you notice the ring on her hand?"

"Sir, I didn't notice . . ."

"She also had a bracelet. Did the bracelet fall off when you chopped her arms off?"

"I didn't chop the woman's arms off."

"Who did?"

"I don't know."

"You don't know who did?"

"I don't"

"Well, let's see if I can refresh your memory. She was in your van with you. She was hitchhiking. You picked her up. You said that. She identified your van. She identified your house. She identified you. She also said that you had a daughter that lived in Reno. She knew your name. You told it to her."

"Now! look—"

"You stopped at the A & W station."

"There's another Larry in this, too." Singleton practically screamed.

"The only problem, you said this Larry's got blond hair, he's got a beard or kinda straggly hair. But see, *you* have brown hair, bushy eyebrows, blue eyes, you have a bigger nose, and you're much older. That's the Larry she identified."

"Well..."

"We saw the picture in the paper. We identified you with that picture in the paper. How do you think all of these things came about and came to you, Mr. Singleton? We know that you did it. What we'd really all like to know is: why?"

"I did not do it. I could not do it."

"Maybe you couldn't do it, but you did it."

"I could not do it."

"Maybe you can't do it again, maybe you can do it again."

"Sir, I could not use a weapon on anybody."

"You might not use a weapon, but you used an ax. She saw you when you reached up and you let it go and you were holding her arm. She saw you cut her two more times and yank that arm off!

"She saw you do it. She saw you pick up that ax and her hand. You grabbed her and you flipped her over and you grabbed the other arm and you cut that one off."

"That's an absolute lie, sir."

"And then afterwards, you cut her loose."

"That's an absolute lie. That woman was never tied up. That woman was never tied up."

"Never tied up?"

"No."

"Well, you covered that up very well 'cause you took her hands, with the rope. Where did you put her hands? Did you throw them in the canal or did you throw them alongside the road?"

"I don't know."

"What did you do with her clothes?"

"I didn't do anything."

"Do you expect me to believe that? Do you expect this detective to believe that, Mr. Singleton?" Breshears said expressionlessly.

"Well, sir, that's all I know."

"Why would two guys who know nothing about your van, but have a gun, take an ax out of your toolbox and use that when all they had to do was shoot her?"

"I can't answer that question."

"Because they weren't even there! You were the only one in that van."

"No, sir."

"Hell, you got scared. You got scared after you had sexual relations with her. You were petrified. You were afraid that she knew too much about you and she could turn you in and catch you and you didn't have any alternative but to get rid of her. You were petrified and you were scared."

"No, I—"

"Admit it!"

"No."

"You would have to be a scared man who would cut a woman's arms off."

"I could not..."

"It would also have to be a scared man after he cut the woman's arms off to make sure that she wasn't dead."

"I'll tell you the God's truth, I did not... mutilate that woman."

"Don't tell me the God's truth, unless you're planning on telling me the whole truth."

"I am telling you the whole truth."

"You're not telling me the truth," Breshears shot back. "You're not only lying to me now, you're lying to God. You're going to go to hell and pay for it, let me tell you."

"Well, I'll tell you the truth..."

"And, you know, Mr. Singleton, you're over fifty years old now. Is that what you want? Is that the way you want it to end?"

"Look, if I thought that I was capable of cutting anybody's arms off... I just can't conceive of it."

"That's why you tried to kill yourself, Mr. Singleton."

"I didn't try to kill myself."

"You just overdosed on pills, and with the combination of liquor, you ended up in the hospital, in the ICU, Mr. Singleton. Why don't you face it? You can't live with it, Mr. Singleton."

"Well..."

"You've got to help yourself now. Now's the time to help yourself."

"All right, now look. You can check it out. I was shook up about having cancer of the throat."

"I know you were shook up and I know something else that really shook you up, Mr. Singleton. That's the fact that the girl lived and you didn't think that she would and you're scared to death. You're shaking right now."

"I... I'm shaking right now. I'll grant you that, because I can't tell you what happened because as far as I know, that girl was alive the last time I seen her. And the last time I seen her, she had her clothes on. Now that's as far as I can tell you. She had her clothes on the last time I saw her."

"Why don't you tell us now? Tell us what happened," Breshears gently implored him.

Breshears leaned forward on the table and examined Singleton.

"You know, she described the color of your eyes perfectly. Light blue."

"Well, I don't understand how..."

"It's funny how she could give such a good description of you and she doesn't even remember anybody else in the van."

"And... I don't understand why she's mad at me..."

Breshears glared at him, beginning to lose patience.

"Maybe 'cause you chopped her arms off! And let me tell you, Mr. Singleton, she's not mad at you. I told you before. She feels sorry for you."

"Well, I'll tell you the God's truth 'cause—"

"She knows what you've got to live through."

"I... I... could not ever do anything like that!"

Breshears wasn't impressed with his denial. "Her arms can be replaced with other devices," he explained, "but your mind can't."

It was not necessarily the best thing to say to a suspect under interrogation that he was, in effect nuts, but Breshears was getting sick and tired of the old mariner's steadfast denials.

"I could not conceivably use a weapon on anybody," Singleton continued to protest.

Breshears smiled. "You couldn't conceivably, but you did. Why? Why don't you tell us?"

"I didn't, I didn't use any weapon!" Singleton screamed.

"An ax is a weapon, Mr. Singleton."

"I know that. I'm not stupid."

Breshears had to wonder.

"I don't know what she's mad at me about. I mean—"

Breshears decided to take another tack. Maybe Singleton would respond better to compassion, no matter how manufactured it was.

"I can realize your not wanting to remember," the cop began gently, "or trying to forget what happened."

"I'm not—"

"Come on, there's got to be a reason that you did it," Reese broke in reasonably.

"I'm not trying to forget anything," Singleton protested. "I'm only telling you as it actually was." Singleton warmed to his topic. "Now I got a gun and a knife there with me in the van. I told you the damn truth about it. I tried to convince those two idiots and I think that I did a good job of that, telling them we should go back to San Francisco. And I told them, all we have to do is go to the bank tomorrow morning and we'll have all the money we need."

"I have a question here," Breshears said dubiously. "You said 'tomorrow morning.' Tomorrow morning was Saturday. Is the bank open down there on Saturday?"

"No."

"Then how come you told them it was open on Saturday?"

"Well . . ."

"Go on, tell us," Reese baited him.

"Well, I had a little trouble talking. But I mean, Larry could have figured that out."

"There's one bank, *one bank* in the whole city that's open day and night. It's on Market Street. That's the Bank of America, that's a day-and-night bank. That's the only one. You didn't point them to that bank. You pointed them to a bank that was going to be closed." Breshears looked down at his notes. "You had pointed them to a bank on Sixth and Mission."

"I showed . . ." Singleton began weakly, and then his voice trailed off. He was caught in a big lie and he knew it.

"You dropped them off at Sixth and Mission after you showed them where the bank was. You said it was one block right there and what street is that bank on?"

"Well, Crocker Bank is on Market over there."

"Yeah, but, hey, that's a long ways from Sixth and Mission."

"No, it's not a long ways."

"Sure it is," Breshears answered brightly. "Where was this bank at on Market Street?"

"It's not on Sixth and Market. It's between Sixth and Seventh there on Market."

"No, it isn't," Breshears shot back. "It's farther, way farther up. It's almost up to where the day-and-night bank is. That's the Bank of America."

"Now, the day-and-night bank is—"

"The Bank of America."

"Yeah."

"That's *seven*, eight blocks farther up the road. You said one block. You specifically said one block. I've written it right here." He showed him the note he'd made on his pad, before continuing. "And you said the bank was one block from Sixth and Mission where you would meet them on Saturday. There's no bank there."

"There's the day-and-night bank is only a block . . ."

Breshears shook his head. "You specifically showed them where that bank was, one block from Sixth and Mission where you dropped them off."

Breshears continued the questioning along these lines, trying to show Singleton that he was lying by catching him in inconsistencies regarding the fabricated directions he gave to "Larry" and "Pedro."

"How could you convince them that you were on the level if you tried to show them where a bank isn't? That's not being on the level, Mr. Singleton."

Singleton looked around like a caged animal, and licked his lips. He was trying to think of a way out of the verbal prison he found himself in. "I know where the day-and-night branch is, too. It's not one block from there. It's several, many blocks from there. And I told them I'd meet them right back there at Sixth and Mission."

Is this the best he can do? the cops thought. Back to this crap?

"See, I wanted them to get out of the car," Singleton explained rationally.

"At Sixth and Mission? Why at Sixth and Mission?"

"Because I could turn around and come back on the freeway," Singleton answered in triumph.

"No, I don't think so." Breshears burst his bubble. "You could have dropped them on Harrison, Howard, any of those streets, just one block away, and as soon as you dropped them off, you could have shot right around the corner and got back on the freeway."

"Well, all I wanted to do was convince them."

"Yes, but how could you do that if you weren't on the level?"

"Well, by that time they were pretty well stoned, too."

"Yeah, but I mean you showed them a building and said, 'That's the bank,' and there wasn't any bank there. And they believed you? Come on!"

"Well, I told them that it wouldn't be good for us to be seen together."

"So you showed them where the bank was that isn't there, and dropped them off at Sixth and Mission one block away?"

"Yeah."

Singleton failed to see the contradiction.

"*But there's no bank there.*"

"I told them the bank was a block up and over."

"You pointed it out to them. You said it was there and it wasn't."

"I didn't point it out. I said it's right over there."

"Why did you pick them up in the first place?" Reese wondered.

Singleton turned and looked at Reese.

"She insisted."

"She already had a stick and a knife and she insisted. You had a gun, of course. And she insisted," said Breshears.

If a person's words could be said to be dripping sarcasm, Breshears's were at that moment.

"But I didn't even know the gun was in the car," Singleton protested. "That's the God's truth!"

65

"You didn't know."

"Yeah."

"The gun . . ."

"Pedro got the gun."

"Pedro got the gun," Breshears repeated. "Where did he get the gun from in the car?"

"I don't know."

Breshears looked at Singleton closely and pointed at his nose. "You know, she even described the little marks right here on your nose. Those little broken blood vessels." *From drinking*, he thought.

"Listen, I don't know what she described, but—"

"Hairy chest."

"But—"

"Over fifty."

"She must have been awful—"

"Receding hairline, balding on top, graying on the sides."

"Gray hair on the chest," Reese added.

"I don't know why she picked me out." Singleton was pleading.

"What are you going to do?" Breshears asked.

"I don't know why she picked me out." And now, Singleton was almost in tears. It was time to move in again.

"Did you do it?" Breshears asked quietly.

"No, I did not do it, sir."

"Yeah, you did it, Mr. Singleton."

"I did not do it, sir! I could not do it."

"You're saying to yourself that you could not do it," said Reese, "but it happened."

"It wasn't me!" Singleton screamed.

"She says that you're the one that did it," Reese answered, looking him straight in the eyes.

"No!"

"You have a fifteen-year-old girl who you say you were afraid of 'cause she had a stick. A man like you that's been in Korea, been in combat, as big and as strong as you are, who likes to fight. And you couldn't take care of one little girl with a stick and a knife?"

"A guy who admits he has a violent temper?" Breshears added.

"You could have stopped at any time and told her to get out, and she would have got out of the van and—"

"She could have stuck me in the eye with that goddamn stick, or in the stomach!"

"How about when you got out and went into that A & W? You were away from her then. Why didn't you go over and dial the phone and send the cops on her?" Reese wondered.

"How about when you went in and paid the money for the tokens at the gas pump," Breshears remembered. "You could have called the cops then."

"I got out of the van three times," Singleton recalled. "Now, she obviously took some pills or something up there in Auburn, because she was a completely different person when she came back in that van. She was violent."

"She's different, too. She's a lot different. For some reason, her arms are a lot shorter than they used to be," said Breshears.

"Now, sir—"

"Three times you got out of the van and three times you had a chance to call the police if you wanted and you didn't," said Reese.

"I did not want to. You see, I picked up many hitchhikers."

"Yeah, but we're talking about this one. Just this one hitchhiker. 'Course, I probably wouldn't have picked her up in the first place. But if I had picked her up, I wouldn't have cut her arms off."

"Well, I did not cut that woman's arms off, sir."

Ignoring him, Reese asked, "Were you mad because she said she'd come to Reno with you and then all of a sudden she wants to go to L.A.?"

"No. I don't want her to come to Reno. I even offered to give her money. I told her, I said, 'Well, if you want to.' She said, 'You're going to drive me to L.A.'"

"Then why did you turn around from above Sacramento," Breshears asked, voice rising, "and start going south?"

"Because she whacked me with a stick."

"Were you going to drive her to L.A.?" Breshears repeated.

"I would have driven her to L.A. if I hadn't of picked up those other two clowns."

"You would have driven her to L.A?"

"Yeah."

"But she whacked you with a stick and it petrified you?"

"No, it didn't, I . . ."

"You weren't scared of her?"

"Look, if you had a sharp stick and you figured that . . ."

"Well, how about three times when you got out of the van? You were a long way from that sharp stick. All you had to do was say, 'Hey, get out of my van or I'll call the police. Hey, somebody, come over here, and watch while I get this woman out of my van.' You didn't do any of those things. You got back in," Breshears accused him.

"She had already—"

"In with that girl with the vicious stick." Breshears was being sarcastic again. "That doesn't make sense, Mr. Singleton. It doesn't make the least amount of sense. Not even a little," he added, shaking his head sadly.

"Sir, could I have some more coffee?" Singleton asked.

What was this, a Folger's commercial, the cops wondered.

"Sure," said Breshears.

Breshears looked at the middle-aged man. On the surface, he seemed harmless enough, but Breshears had seen his grisly handiwork. And that's why Breshears just wasn't going to give up. He wanted a confession, and by God, he was going to get it.

SIX

The press was there at Modesto's airport to greet Jaime Sommers when she stepped out of her Learjet. She had come to Modesto to visit with Mary Vincent, whom she passionately identified with.

Sommers was also a young woman, though in her twenties. Her injuries, however, had been worse than Mary's: she had lost both legs and both arms due to a sky-diving accident.

She would have been left a helpless cripple had it not been for her friend Steve Austin. Austin, an astronaut, had lost his limbs in a horrible accident, too. But they had been replaced with bionic members that gave him ten times the strength and agility he had had. It had cost six million dollars to put Austin together again. It would cost just about the same to fit Sommers with bionic limbs, but Austin convinced the super-secret government agency he worked for to help Jaime.

Austin's doctor, Rudy Wells, was called in to oversee the reconstruction, and when Jaime awakened, she, too, had lifelike bionic limbs and, most importantly, no deformities. Reporters were aware of her history as Jaime climbed out of the two-seater. They stared at her in awe, but not at her bionic limbs.

Jaime Sommers was actually a fictitious character, the heroine of a popular TV series on NBC called *The Bionic Woman*. The actress who played the part was Lindsay Wagner, and it was Lindsay, not

Jaime, who climbed out of that plane to pay a hospital call on Mary Vincent.

Some people thought it was ludicrous—a Hollywood actress, who played a woman with prosthetic limbs, trying to relate to a woman who was being fitted for them. The line between reality and entertainment had blurred.

Miles away from the hospital, as Wagner spent four hours trying to give Mary what help she could, Breshears looked Singleton straight in the eye.

"You know, you only tell us the truth up to a point."

Singleton frowned.

"Yeah, you do," the cop continued. "You're afraid to tell us the rest." He leaned closer, crowding Singleton into the corner. "Why don't you tell us the rest of what happened?" he asked softly.

"I don't know, now as far as I know, that girl just got out of the van," Singleton sputtered.

"You know what happened," Breshears answered. "You do know what happened."

"*I do not know what happened*," Singleton protested.

"What did she do to scare you," Breshears continued, "to the point where you had to cut her arms off? What did she say? What did she do to make you do that?"

Singleton thought for a moment. "I did not cut that woman's arms off, sir," he answered politely.

"They're gone," Breshears reminded him. "And these two phantoms, Larry and Pedro, weren't there because you never picked them up. Isn't that right?"

If this had been television, it would have been the point where the TV cop leans in menacingly and begins to rough the suspect up a bit to get a confession. But in real life, if that was done, the judge would throw the case out because the suspect's constitutional rights had been violated. All Breshears could do was keep up the verbal and psychological pressure, and hope Singleton would crack.

"Well, I'll tell you guys the truth about it. It seems like I'm taking the rough end of this all day."

"Yeah, so why not be truthful?" Breshears asked.

"Truthfully, I don't understand this myself," Singleton responded in a rather perplexed manner. It was as though he was saying, "Why bother me? I'm a good guy. I pay my taxes. Why don't you go out and get a real bad guy?"

"Well, if you don't understand it, I certainly don't," Breshears continued. "I want to know what would make a man so afraid that he would try to get rid of her? She had to say something, to do something to you. What did she say or what did she do to cause you to do that?"

"But I wasn't angry with the girl!" Singleton denied vociferously. It was beginning to sink in how much trouble he was really in if he couldn't convince this cop of his innocence.

"You had to be scared then," said Breshears.

"In fact, I was actually . . ."

It had been a moment of truth, but Singleton faltered and backtracked. "I figured we'd all go back to San Francisco, I'd dump them off, and I'd get some sleep."

Breshears reminded him that, "If she'd been holding a stick on you, she would have probably hit you with it again if you started to go to San Francisco." She had wanted L.A.

"I told her that she started playing Larry off against me and that's when I figured, 'Now I'm in real trouble.'"

"Did she threaten you with the stick any more?"

"No, she told Larry that I'd been bugging her."

"How do you mean 'bugging her'?"

"She insinuated that—"

"What were her words?" Reese interrupted him.

"I've forgotten now, sir. I'll try to recall later. But at any rate, there's a five-or six-inch hunting knife laying there in the brown bag I keep in the van."

"Did she just reach down and open it up and pull the knife out?"

"Yeah, she did." Singleton nodded vigorously.

"How did she know it was in there?"

"Because the bag was wide open."

"Do you always keep the bag wide open? That's funny, because when we saw it today, it was closed."

"Well, normally, like I said, what I did was just throwed the junk in the car and that's exactly what I did, throw that junk in the car. The bag was just laying there open."

"Man, the bag was closed," Breshears contradicted him.

"The bag was open in the van," Singleton corrected him.

"You reached in, you got the knife out, and you cut the ropes off of her hands."

"That's a lie, sir!"

"It isn't a lie. We got the rope out there—it's been cut."

"To my knowledge, that girl never had any ties on her. In fact, she's the one that wanted to stay stoned."

"Right, and you found out how old she was and you got scared afterwards. Isn't that the way it was?"

"I did not know how old she was."

"She's fifteen years old. Fifteen."

"Now, she told me she was . . ."

"Fifteen years old," Breshears repeated.

"Almost twenty-one," Singleton insisted.

"And no arms, no hands," Breshears added.

"Well, sir, I could not cut anybody's arms off."

"You couldn't, unless you were scared enough, and you were. Why were you so scared?"

"I was not scared," Singleton protested again. "I was not."

Breshears leaned across the table and Singleton could feel his breath.

"What made you so scared?" Breshears whispered.

"Actually, for a while, I was frightened," Singleton admitted. It was the first time he had clearly indicated fear at all. "But," the merchant marine continued, "like I say, I did pull those checks out."

"Then you weren't scared. You did it because you thought she would die in that pipe. And she didn't die. She crawled out and walked away."

Singleton didn't answer.

"It's obvious that you never did anything like that before, or you would have seen that she wasn't dead. But you were too scared. You left in too big of a hurry, because you were too scared for what you did."

"Sir, I don't even know when the girl got out of the van. In fact, we all got out about four times."

"You helped her out of the van, Mr. Singleton," Breshears answered. "You helped her out of the van and you were petrifying her. You didn't know what to do."

"Sir, that's not right!"

"It is right! She watched you cut her arms off!"

"That is wrong!"

"Why'd you do it?"

"I did not do it," Singleton repeated.

"What did she do? What happened to make you that scared or that angry?"

"I did not take that girl out of the van. Now, we all got out of that van two or three times."

"Uh-huh," Breshears said dubiously.

"Including me," Singleton added.

"And one time," Breshears corrected him, "she didn't get back in the van, and it was just you and her and the ax there."

"No, sir, absolutely not."

"That's all that was there. No one else."

"Absolutely not, sir."

"You know, you shouldn't lie about something like that."

"I'm not lying!"

"If somebody chopped your arms off and there were three people, wouldn't you pick the right one? Wouldn't you identify the right person? Wouldn't you?"

"If she identified me, she's wrong."

"When you got rid of her hands, did you notice that ring on them?"

"I did not get rid of her hands."

"Where did that ring go?" Breshears wondered.

"I don't know. I don't even know if it's the same girl or not, except for what has been said here. For the last time, I do not know what you're talking about. I've told you everything I know."

"Except for one thing."

"What?"

Breshears pulled out a picture from under his pad and showed it to Singleton.

"Is that the hand?"

Singleton looked at it for a moment. It was a picture of a severed hand sitting on a rock in San Francisco Bay.

"I cannot..."

"That the hand there?" Breshears pointed to the pale object on the rock.

"I beg your pardon?"

"Is this the hand that you cut off with the ax?"

"No, sir. If there's some blood on that hatchet, I don't know where it came from. I have no way in God's world of knowing, but I couldn't do it."

"Maybe you can explain how it happened. Maybe you don't know how it happened. Maybe you don't know why it happened. That I can understand. I can understand that. She can understand that, too."

Breshears tried sympathy again. Maybe Singleton would respond to sympathy this time and crack.

"Sir, I am fifty years old."

"Mr. Singleton, you've got to help yourself now," Breshears said, a newfound urgency in his words.

"No..."

"It's time for you to help yourself."

"I'll tell you the God's truth, if I could help myself, I would. But I can't say anything that I don't know to be true."

"You can help yourself, though, right now."

"I can't help myself by saying I did something that I know isn't true."

"But you did do it."

Breshears started shuffling his papers, as though he was ready to leave.

"Now there's no way in God's world that I can pull ... use a gun ... of course, now ..." Singleton sputtered.

"You didn't use a gun," Breshears corrected him. "You used an ax."

THE MAD CHOPPER

"Well, I . . ."

"You took it out of your van. It was in your toolbox. You took it out. You were scared. You took the ax out and you cut her hands off so we could never find her fingerprints when she died. That would make identifying her body almost impossible."

"No . . ."

"But you were so scared, you didn't see if she . . ."

"No!"

" . . . was dead. You threw her down the gully. You kicked her, because you were scared."

"I . . ."

"You kicked her into the pipe and kicked her with your foot. Shoved her right in where you figured she'd die."

"I did not kick anybody into a pipe."

"Really? Then how did she get in there? She didn't crawl in there by herself."

"I don't even know anything about a pipe."

"Yes, you do."

"And I—"

"That's the pipe that comes down and goes underneath the road. Did you know that she heard you drive off?"

Singleton's face drained of color.

"Sir . . ."

"She didn't even lose consciousness, and she heard you drive off. That's amazing isn't it? Can you imagine the pain that she was going through at the time, and was still eager to hear you drive off?"

"The only thing I can say is that girl must—"

"Must have a strong will to live," Breshears cut him off.

"No, she must . . . something else is wrong . . . I don't know what . . ."

"Did she lie about her hands and arms? Of course, she might lie about that."

"Sir?" Singleton didn't get it.

"But she told an awful good story, because I know. I looked at them and I didn't see hands there. I didn't see forearms there. I saw one elbow. I saw her when they brought her in from the ambulance with one bone sticking out alone there."

"Well, sir, I don't know . . ."

"You don't know?"

"I can't tell you something else except that I've told you right now. I did not mutilate that girl in any way, shape, or form. She told me that she wanted to stay stoned all her life."

As if that explained her injuries. Or justified them.

"Tell me, when she gave you that blow job, did you reach a climax?"

"I don't remember."

"You don't remember?"

"No, I don't."

"You really don't."

"She sat down on top of me, too," Singleton added.

"And you don't remember a simple detail like if you reached a climax or not?" Breshears sounded incredulous.

"And then Pedro was the one that was goosing her at the time."

"Ah, the mysterious Pedro. Now wait a minute. Somebody's got to be behind the wheel if you and Pedro are going at her."

"I told you we were stopped at that time."

"Oh? You stopped there pretty close to where she got her arms cut off."

"No!"

"You weren't there? You went further down the canyon, laid down next to her . . ."

"Oh, for Christ's sake!"

" . . . told her she would be all right if she did what you said. We're talking about in the canyon. You remember now. In the canyon where you and her were together."

"I never went in any canyon."

"This is the second time. This is the second time that you were going to have sexual intercourse with her. You kind of laid there next to her a little bit. You even got into the van after having sexual intercourse the first time and drove up there with no clothes because you were going to do it again."

"That's an outright lie! She's lying!"

"That's the truth, Mr. Singleton. The real truth. Why don't you tell us the real truth?"

"I never had all my clothes off."
"Sure you did."
"I never did."
"You took your shoes off."
"I did not!"
"You even took your socks off."

As Breshears had enunciated every step of the rape, Singleton had gone paler and paler. But his mouth said, "No, sir, I did not."

"And you took these clothes, your good ones, all the way off."

"No, sir, I didn't."

It was no use. It just wasn't working and both cops knew it. Singleton wasn't cracking.

Breshears said, "Mr. Singleton, we're going to stop and let you get another cup of coffee, because you've asked for one a couple of times and we didn't get it for you. We'd like to talk to you one more time. Not tonight though."

"I . . . uh . . ."

"Now relax, take it easy. Get up in the morning and have breakfast or something and take a good shower."

"Okay."

"And we'd like to talk to you a little bit more tomorrow, but I think maybe we should end it right now. Okay?"

"Yeah, fine."

And the interview was over.

The cops had failed to get a confession. They knew that any further interrogation would probably get them nowhere, especially if Singleton had time to think about what he'd say. There really was no choice, unless they wanted to go all night and listen to Singleton's repeated denials. One thing, though, was certain.

Either he had had an alcoholic blackout when he cut the girl's arms off or he was the most cold-hearted son of a bitch they had ever met.

PART TWO
NO MAN'S LAND

SEVEN

The short film opened with a young girl being wheeled on a gurney into a hospital emergency room. A "Dr. Carter" runs to her aid and begins shouting orders to nearby nurses and orderlies.

In the next scene, the same young girl is out on a deserted highway, hitchhiking. Shortly, she is picked up by a man driving a blue van. As the van drives off, the audience knows what is in her future. On comes the crawl, "Don't be a pigeon," intoned by an offscreen announcer.

Ironically, the public service commercial advising young girls not to hitchhike had been filmed prior to Mary Vincent's assault, and had just begun airing. The use of an actress who looked a lot like Mary, plus her assailant driving a blue van, literally foreshadowed the real-life events.

While the wheels of justice turned, the real Mary Vincent lay in a hospital bed, recovering from her ordeal. With her medical costs likely to exceed $10,000, attention began to focus on how to help her.

California maintained a state program to help victims of violent crimes. The problem was, Mary was not a resident of California, but of Nevada. Regardless of the fact that she had lived in California with Diego, because she was a minor meant that her official place of residence was determined by where her parents resided, and that was

Nevada. California residency was required to receive assistance from the program, which meant Mary's bad luck might be holding.

The horrific crime had focused nationwide attention on California and the state did not want to seem like an insensitive place. It was bad for business.

"Let her family file for assistance. We'd rather lean over backwards and do everything possible for them," said a spokesman for the State Board of Control, which oversaw the victim's assistance program.

Mary's mother, Lucy Vincent, had arrived at the hospital to comfort her daughter. She told the press that the family did have some medical insurance, but she wasn't certain of the exact coverage. There was no question that any assistance the state offered would help.

Private contributions to help with Mary's medical costs had not been generous. They only totaled $300. Additional contributions, however, were still coming in and it was hoped they would be substantial enough to make an impact on her medical bills.

That left the eventual cost of her new arms, which would climb into the thousands, too. Perhaps some generous benefactor would come forward to help with that. Or maybe the state could find it in its heart to aid Mary, because without those arms, she would be left with two sawed-off stumps and helpless. But before any of this could happen, there was something Mary Vincent had to do first.

THURSDAY, OCTOBER 27, 1978

For over an hour, during a three-hour-and-twenty minute closed session, Mary Vincent testified before the Stanislaus County grand jury. She remained calm about the details leading up to the crime, but showed emotion when talking about the attack. A few times she came close to breaking down, but she kept going until she got to the end of her story. As for the people hearing her story, the grand jurors, they struggled to listen to her words and look into her eyes, rather than gazing at her heavily bandaged lower arms.

"I think she displayed a lot of courage" in testifying, District Attorney Donald Stahl said after her testimony. "I think she showed a lot of courage throughout this whole damn thing."

Stahl said that there was no credence to the charge Singleton had leveled against Mary—that she had accepted money from him for sex—nor was there any evidence to back up Singleton's assertion that in addition to Mary, he had picked up the two mysterious hitchhikers, "Larry" and "Pedro."

Other witnesses who testified were Todd Meadows, the motorist who had picked Mary up bleeding by the side of the road outside Del Puerto Canyon, and Detective Reese, who read the statement Singleton had made at the time of his arrest. Singleton himself did not appear, since the defendant does not have to appear during grand jury proceedings.

It does not take much for a prosecutor to get an indictment from a grand jury, since it is the state itself that calls the grand jury together. All the rules of evidence are set up in the state's favor. While there are times when the grand jury refuses to indict, in the Singleton case, given the weight of the evidence, it would have been a major surprise if the grand jury had not come back with a positive result.

Shortly after retiring to consider the evidence, the Stanislaus County grand jury reached its conclusion. Singleton was brought in for the formal reading of the indictment in front of Superior Court Judge Francis W. Halley. Concerned, lest someone with a grudge, or some nut might try to make a name for himself by killing Singleton, Sheriff Lynn Wood put on lots of extra security.

Accompanying Singleton into court were more than a dozen sheriff's deputies, who were posted around the defendant and throughout the courtroom. Deputies stood guard in the outside corridor. Court spectators had gone through metal detectors on the way into the courtroom, and no one was allowed within a distance of ten feet of Singleton as he was escorted through the corridor that connected the prisoners' elevator and Judge Halley's courtroom.

When he arrived in court, Singleton took his place by the defense table. Only a few reporters and photographers were present, because Stahl had carried on the grand jury proceedings behind closed doors to avoid a media circus. Encased in security leg chains and handcuffs, attired in orange jail coveralls, Singleton, head bowed, silently read a copy of the charges as the clerk read them out loud.

"Lawrence Singleton, you are charged with one count of forcible rape, two counts of forcible copulation, one count of sodomy, one count of kidnapping, one count of mayhem, and one count of attempted murder." That made a total of seven charges in all.

Bail was set at $200,000. A Florida attorney, Henry Gonzalez, informed District Attorney Donald Stahl that he would represent Singleton, along with a California lawyer yet to be retained. It was rumored that Singleton had family in Florida that was paying for his legal representation.

In the wake of the attack, alcohol abuse experts were consulted by the police and prosecutors. Their overriding question was this: could a person in an alcoholic blackout commit the kind of crime Singleton had and have no memory of it afterward?

If the answer came back "yes," it would give Singleton a diminished capacity defense at trial. If the answer was "no," Singleton would have to convince a jury of twelve men and women that "Larry" and "Pedro" existed and they were the ones who had committed the crime.

Thankfully, for the prosecution, the answer came back an unqualified "no."

In the opinion of the alcohol abuse experts, a person could not have hacked off a girl's arms while in the throes of an alcoholic blackout and not have any memory of it later. Instead, the alcohol would act as a triggering mechanism, releasing the pent-up rage and sadistic impulses that dwelled just below the surface of a person's consciousness. Released from his ego, his id would be free to act up. Or out. Or cut.

Interestingly, while heavy drinkers or just occasional drinkers could suffer blackouts where they were not aware of their actions in general, alcohol could not erase an individual's moral code. In other words, if Singleton thought it wrong while sober to cut someone's arms off, he would feel the same way during the blackout. Likewise, if violence suited him sober, it would suit him drunk. In either case, the individual was still responsible for his actions. Which suited the cops and D.A. just fine.

They had Singleton where they wanted him. Let him make his case for "Pedro" and "Larry" and they'd see if the jury would buy his story.

It had been Sondra Ruben's tip that had led the cops to capture Singleton and, as usual, the reporters wanted to hear from the hero of the hour, ignoring the detective work of Breshears and Reese.

"I suffered over this decision," she told the media. "I wasn't sure I'd done the right thing after I called."

The housewife and mother of five did not know until after she'd called in her tip that an anonymous person had offered a $5,000 reward for information leading to the arrest and conviction of the suspect.

"That's good, I'm glad, because I was worried that the money had come from the family," Sondra said.

What Breshears and Reese did not know was they had a rather accomplished sailor on their hands. As far as the United States Coast Guard was concerned, Lawrence Singleton was qualified to command any United States merchant marine ship on the high seas, anything from a two-hundred-ton tanker filled with oil to the *Queen Elizabeth II* cruise ship, which transported thousands of passengers every month. In fact, the cops had a real prodigy on their hands, a man who was known as an "unlimited master," the highest ranking the Coast Guard could bestow on a sailor. In order to get that rating, a sailor must have many years of sailing experience and pass a series of detailed examinations. The exams lasted four full days.

Singleton had been a most ambitious man. Even those with a master's rating needed to study hard at a maritime college before they could move up to unlimited master. Singleton had, taking his formal training in 1974 at the Maritime Institute of Technology and Graduate Studies in Baltimore. Ever the overachiever, he graduated with a captain's certificate.

"Even with schooling, not all pass," said Jace Beemer, a spokesman for the Coast Guard's Maritime Safety Office in San Francisco. "Some applicants just give up. But if they are motivated, they go after it. On the section of the exam called 'Rules of the Sea,' it takes a grade of ninety percent to pass, and on other parts of the exam, seventy percent is required."

Singleton was proficient in the rules of the sea, navigation, techniques of ship operation, and radar equipment, and even in such arcane details as how to balance the oil in a tanker so the ship wouldn't list.

As Lawrence Singleton's arrest flashed across the news wires, in no place was it received more sadly than in New Orleans. New Orleans had been Singleton's home base for years. Like his fellow mates, he would wait in the seamen's union hall for word from shippers that they needed mates. When he found one that required his services, he signed on immediately and shipped out to ports worldwide.

Authorities suspected that Singleton's attack on Mary Vincent was not an isolated incident. He had been accused of assaulting his daughter, too, and speculation arose that if police had the time and resources to check his activities in faraway ports, they would find that he had assaulted women in those places, too. Unfortunately, if a record of violence existed somewhere else, no one knew where it was, nor did they have the resources to obtain it.

In his home port of New Orleans, though, no one knew of any charges against him. By 1968, he was ready for a change and he moved to the San Francisco Bay Area, where he took a position with the American President Lines out of Oakland.

Singleton seemed to acclimate himself quite well to the line's cruise ships. He fraternized with female crew members who caught his fancy, which was how, one day in 1970, aboard the line's *President Wilson*, he happened to meet Celia Johnson. At the time, Singleton was the ship's navigator and Celia the ship's nurse. Celia found the rugged seaman attractive. Singleton, who had been married and was divorced with a teenage daughter named Debbie, thought Celia was the one for him. They eventually married.

Soon after that, Singleton left cruise ships and hired on to the Central Gulf Lines, once again out of New Orleans. This put a strain on his marriage, basing himself in New Orleans while his wife lived on the West Coast. But by that time, Celia had realized she was involved with a guy who not only drank too much, but was violent when he got drunk. That was much more than she had bargained for.

While Celia tried to figure out what to do, Singleton found himself as chief mate, second in command, on the *Green Wave*. Under contract for the Military Sealift Command her cargo was ammunition bound for Vietnam.

While Henry Kissinger had brokered a peace agreement to end the Vietnam War in December 1972, that didn't stop the stockpiling of arms. Thus Singleton found himself transporting ammo into a war zone. The assignment brought back memories of another war from a long time ago that he had participated in.

Singleton had served with distinction as an infantryman in Korea. Some of his friends said that he had participated in the most famous and bloody battle of the "police action"—Pork Chop Hill.

Pork Chop Hill was a vicious frontal assault up and across rocky terrain by American soldiers. Gunning for them were Communist Chinese troops. Because it was a frontal assault, the American casualties totaled over fifty percent. As the Americans' ammo ran out, they were forced into vicious hand-to-hand fighting with the enemy. It was an experience that Singleton rarely, if ever, spoke about. There was good reason to assume that his war experiences had left him with what is now known as post-traumatic stress disorder.

Up until the Vietnam War, it was called shell shock, and treatment was little and intermittent because it was not acknowledged to be a long-standing problem. But as the veterans of the Vietnam War would show, post-traumatic stress disorder, an adverse reaction in civilian life to the stress soldiers face under fire, could completely destroy an individual's life in peacetime. Had such knowledge, and advanced treatment, which included talking therapy and administering anti-depressant medication, been available to Singleton, Mary Vincent might still have two whole arms.

It was therefore not surprising that Singleton and his wife, Celia, had so many problems that they eventually divorced. But they still saw each other frequently.

"What more is a divorce than a neon chapel wedding?" Celia would later tell a newspaperman.

Meanwhile, aboard the *Green Wave*, Singleton touched anchor in Da Nang, Saigon, Guam, Midway Island, Korea, Okinawa, Taiwan, and Yokohama. In 1975, he sailed through the locks of the Panama Canal, gazed silently at Gaillard Cut, the vast expanse of the canal, where the air is haunted by the dead who fell there from Yellow Fever, and then up the eastern coast of Texas and back to New Orleans.

Time to move again. He had these wandering sea legs. The *Green Wave* was left in his wake as he climbed aboard the *S.S. Green Valley*, another Central Gulf ship. The ship transported cargo to Northern Europe and Singleton soon found himself sailing through the Red Sea and the Persian Gulf.

Singleton seemed to have a death wish. With his rating, he could have stayed above deck in a more administrative position, but he chose to become a tanker mate, one of the most dangerous jobs aboard any vessel. Much time was spent below decks, breathing poisonous fumes in the presence of gallons and gallons of flammable oil.

Singleton's job as chief mate was to supervise the loading and unloading of oil, a job that came with its inherent career dangers, for if any of that oil should spill and he was found responsible, he could face criminal as well as civil penalties. Ironically, given his propensity to consume alcohol, he was never found drunk on duty and had a spotless record. This was despite the fact that his duty required him to work seven days a week for months on end. Clearly, he stayed sober while working.

As for money, Singleton had not been lying when he said he had it. Singleton made approximately $3,000 per month, with room and board provided. By the time he mutilated Mary Vincent, he had enough money stowed away to buy another couple of homes if he wanted, and another couple of vans.

He was ready to retire and enjoy the rest of his life. Then, in his opinion, he made the mistake of picking up that stupid bitch on the highway and everything went haywire.

Among those who were upset over Singleton's arrest was his ex-wife Celia Johnson. Turned out, she lived across town from Singleton in Sparks, in a large apartment complex. Singleton had moved to Sparks some ten years before on the advice of a merchant seaman friend who told him it was a nice place to live.

"He couldn't have done it," Celia told a local paper. "It was not his style." And then she went on to paint a picture of Lawrence Singleton directly at odds with his violent public persona.

Celia told of his devotion to his first wife, Shirley, who had died from cancer two years before. Unlike most seagoing men, her Larry was faithful to her. He was also a father who took pride in his offspring, boasting frequently of Debbie, who would soon be sixteen.

Sixteen being the legal age to drive in California, her loving father had just purchased her a brand-new Ford Thunderbird as an early birthday present. The girl also had two horses and everything a young girl could want. Yet for all that she had, there was much trouble between them.

Debbie and Singleton had argued over the ownership of the Bay-Area home that was still in her mom, Shirley's, name. Singleton had been drinking and his rage surfaced. After it did, Debbie was left with her father's handprint across the side of her face where he had slapped her. Debbie then turned to the law for relief.

She lodged a complaint against Singleton, claiming he drank too much, and when he did, she was afraid of being beaten. She wanted to be removed from his custody, free to move in with some friends in Sparks.

"It all started about three months ago," Celia continued. "He just didn't seem to find any sense with life anymore."

Singleton suffered from depression, which apparently remained untreated. His health began to fail. A chest ailment ballooned in his mind to cancer. Celia thought it came from breathing in too many noxious fumes below decks. He did have skin cancer from his years of seagoing and remaining out on deck, exposed to the sun's deadly rays. But what was most telling was what had happened to Singleton in the week after his assault on Mary Vincent.

Apparently, his conscience got the better of him. Singleton combined scotch and barbiturates in a particularly lethal cocktail that he imbibed to commit suicide. Whatever demons were haunting him had overwhelmed him and he just wanted to check out. But he didn't succeed—he wound up in the hospital instead, where he stayed for four days while he recovered. When he was released, he read a story in the Sunday newspaper about the ax-rapist search.

Carefully, Celia recalled, he folded the newspaper, then quietly sat holding it for some time. Celia figured he was just suffering from stress and exhaustion. Yet back in her mind, she remembered numerous times he had picked up hitchhikers, including one time when she was frightened by some disreputable characters he had picked up. And there was another time when he showed his passion for "eye-for-an-eye" justice. On that occasion, they were driving toward Reno, when a male hitchhiker he happened to pick up pulled a knife and robbed him.

"Take off your clothes and get out," the knife-wielding hitchhiker ordered. Singleton's hand flashed down under his seat. It came up with a loaded revolver and Singleton turned the tables.

"Now *you* take off your clothes, get out, and walk," he ordered the hitchhiker.

Some time later, Singleton checked with the sheriff's office. The nude man had been picked up by the cops. Apparently, that incident had just been a prelude to what followed.

Because of extensive pretrial publicity in Stanislaus County, Lawrence Singleton's trial was moved south to San Diego. He finally went on trial in March 1979.

During the trial, Mary, who was then sixteen, testified to the assault and mutilation that Singleton had inflicted on her. Detail by detail, she told the jury how Singleton had violated and mutilated her. By the time she finished, she was tired and limp from the memories that had returned to stalk her once again. Despite that it was in the name of justice and convicting her abuser, she still relived what had happened, and it was truly a trip into hell. Again. Would it ever end?

On March 29, 1979, a California Superior Court jury found Lawrence Singleton guilty of seven counts—one count each of rape, sodomy, kidnapping, mayhem, and attempted murder, and two counts of forcible oral copulation. The state had recently passed new sentencing laws under which the most Singleton could be sentenced to was fourteen years, four months in prison. The judge, seeing no mitigating circumstances, sentenced him to the maximum.

Unfortunately, under those same laws he could be out in eight years with good behavior. As Singleton was being led out of the San Diego courtroom to serve his sentence, all his victim could hope for was that he was a *very* bad boy in prison.

It was as if her life had stopped. Fifteen years old and *bam*, she was frozen in time. That was what life was like for Mary Vincent after the assault.

There were the physical effects of the assault to get over, and the fitting of her new arms, of course, but the real damage was to her psyche. Nothing for her would ever be the same again. Life would never be so safe or precious or beautiful or full of hope. Lawrence Singleton had taken all that from her and more. He would always loom on the horizon to remind her of what her life was, and what it might have been had she never heard his name.

Every morning she woke up, all she had to do was gaze down at her stumps and there was Singleton. There was no getting away from him except at night sometimes, when the artificial arms were taken off and sleep finally overtook her.

When they were removed by her mother or father, or whoever helped her, she was helpless. She could not open a door if the wind blew it shut. If there was a fire, she couldn't open a window to get out. She couldn't answer a phone, or do something she used to take for granted, like wiping herself when she went to the bathroom.

And what was she to do when she got older and applied for a job? Who would hire someone with hooks for hands? To them, she would just be a freak. She saw people's stares when she went out. That was what Singleton had done to her.

He had made her a target of people's prejudices toward the handicapped. He had made her helpless, reduced to relying on others for her basic needs and safety. She had just been flowering into an independent woman, and now, that was gone.

Her future. That's what he had taken away. Her future. And there was no way to retrieve what might have been.

"It isn't fair," she said. "When the sentence was announced, I felt like getting up and strangling him."

But she didn't have hands so she couldn't strangle him. Her hooks, though, could do even more damage, and if he ever came near her again...

EIGHT

1986

San Luis Obispo is a charming seaside community in northern California. Off Highway 101, which ran along the coastline, the surf pounded the unusual rock formations in the harbor offering a picture-perfect view from the hills above the town.

In those hills is the California Men's Colony at San Luis Obispo. "Men's Colony" was a euphemism for prison. It was there that the state chose to warehouse Lawrence Singleton while he was its guest.

In many ways, jail suited Larry Singleton quite well. He was a perfect prisoner. Used to a chain of command in the merchant marines, he respected the prison guards and never gave them any trouble. He was neither young nor good looking, and therefore did not need to worry about attacks by the "sisters," prison slang for homosexuals. As for the rest, if he got into an argument, he could give as good as he got, which therefore meant arguments were at a minimum.

In short, Lawrence Singleton's prison stay was downright boring. He passed his time like most prisoners, wandering aimlessly from day to day, filling any job that the prison ordered him to do—be it in the commissary or machine shop. His last job behind bars was as a student aide in an educational program. Under a 1983 work-incentive law, passed while he was incarcerated, inmates in the program were granted one day off for each day in the program. Of course, Singleton was eligible, and that further cut his sentence.

It would have been smart for the state to require that he attend Alcoholics Anonymous meetings, but the law under which he was originally sentenced did not require that he seek counseling for his alcohol addiction. Never mind that it was the root cause of the violence he had perpetrated on Mary Vincent. Never mind that he might be suffering from post-traumatic stress disorder from his war days.

The law was more concerned with retribution than rehabilitation. Sheltered away from the public, his addiction to alcohol, and violence, smoldered.

Still, no matter what kind of problems Singleton suffered from, they were no excuse for his violence. He was a man who refused to take responsibility for his actions, and others had continually covered up for him over the years. Otherwise, he could never have reached fifty with a record that had remained spotless until the Vincent tragedy. By 1986, he was a fifty-nine-year-old rapist about to be paroled.

With time off for good behavior and the points he accumulated as a student aide, Singleton was now scheduled to be paroled in April 1987. He would have served eight years of his fourteen-year sentence. But the singular nature of Singleton's crime made him much more a part of the public's consciousness than any single malefactor in California state prison history.

All the while he was in jail, public sentiment had been building against him. Politicians in particular were outraged that his parole was coming up, and none more so than the man who had prosecuted him, Stanislaus County District Attorney Donald Stahl. Said Stahl: "He got the maximum sentence [yet] even the judge said he wished he could've give him life. The work-incentive law is a terrible one, but that's the law, unfortunately."

How heinous the assault was didn't matter. As far as the law was concerned, assault was assault, until the law was changed. As for where Singleton would go after his parole, Stahl wanted him to stay out of Stanislaus County.

"It doesn't make a whit of sense to send him here. There's nothing he wants in Stanislaus County; he's a merchant seaman," the D.A. said, trying to convince himself, and perhaps reassure his constituents that the last place where the master seaman would ever want to settle was in landlocked Modesto.

The chief of the state parole office in Modesto, Leonard Olives, told the *San Jose Mercury News*, that he would recommend that Singleton be paroled elsewhere, "Because he had such a high notoriety."

Singleton was not exactly the most popular visitor Modesto had ever had. In other words, there were people who wouldn't mind seeing him dead if he came back to the same town that he elevated from simple anonymity to the site of what was now viewed as the worst assault in California state history.

In between his work-release assignment and other prison duties, Lawrence Singleton learned the one immutable rule of prison life: there are no guilty men in prison.

Caught killing your wife?

"She killed herself. I was just there watching."

Embezzled money from your employer?

"It was just a loan that I meant to pay back."

Raped a girl and cut off her arms?

"I was framed!"

Singleton had said that at the time of his arrest and he decided to stick to his story. In his cell, crowded with appeal letters, trial transcripts, and other documents pertinent to his case, Singleton decided to give an interview to a reporter from the *San Jose Mercury News*, in which he vociferously proclaimed his innocence.

"Why doesn't the media look at what happened?" an angry and frustrated Singleton demanded. He produced typewritten documents from his case, stabbing his finger at specific sections.

"It was an inquisition," he continued, "an inquisition! There was only the word of the accuser and nothing else." As for his trial in San Diego, he characterized it as "a farce and a scam."

Singleton went on to claim that "mental torture" was inflicted on him while being held in jail at San Diego. He was held "in the 3-G tank without any lights, and cockroaches running in my ear until I finally got moved. I wasn't allowed a full night's sleep either. I don't see how I kept my sanity. They took my mind away from me."

Despite the fact that he had no hard evidence to support his charges, Singleton continued to go on the attack.

What was his version of the night that Mary Vincent lost her arms? Once again, he claimed that he picked up two male hitchhikers and that they had been responsible for cutting Mary Vincent's arms off, not him. He insisted that after they had passed Sacramento, Mary got so angry at him for missing the cutoff to Los Angeles that he tried to kick her out of the van when they reached Auburn.

"She [Vincent] was smoking PCP and she got foul mouthed." He failed to say how a sailor could be offended by anyone's cursing. "I can't stand that kind of talk from a woman. Anyway, I gave her five dollars and told her to get going. But she sees my twenties and changed her mind, and that's when she put a stick to my neck and tells me she wants to go to Los Angeles and she won't cry rape."

Singleton failed to show how anyone in history ever had their life truly threatened by a stick to the neck. But he, a veteran, was afraid of the deadly stick to the neck and the little girl wielding it. The former serviceman and merchant marine turned tail and headed south as the girl demanded. Then Singleton told a wild tale that he hadn't even made up for Breshears or Reese.

Near Galt, just south of Sacramento, Vincent started ripping her clothes off. She was a nymphomaniac. When they stopped at a drive-in restaurant a short time later, he told her one more time to get lost. She defied his order. It was shortly after that that he picked up the two hitchhikers, "Larry" and "Pedro." Now, she figured she'd get lots of action. At least, that was Singleton's version of events.

Commenting on the disposition of his case, he claimed that the investigators had framed him by putting a hatchet in his toolbox. As for the bloody pants they had recovered, he said that they never existed. And the washed carpet in the rear of his van? Well, he washed it because his teenage daughter had been hauling hay for a horse he had bought her.

None of it was true, but who knew, maybe someone would bite? It was certainly a more plausible story than the one he had told Breshears and Reese.

If his lies wouldn't do the trick, maybe, he figured, he could use facts to help himself.

Singleton not only denied assaulting Mary, he claimed that he had never raped her. Strangely, a lab report of a sperm sample taken from Vincent did not match his blood type. Singleton said that the lab report was never introduced at trial by his lawyer.

Never mind that there could be a myriad of reasons why the sample didn't match his blood type. He could have been impotent.

After he had pushed all the buttons that showed he was an innocent, maligned man, it was time to trot out a plea for sympathy. That was another trick he'd learned in prison: make 'em feel sorry for you. Singleton said he was destitute, completely broke, and Debbie, his loving daughter, had been adversely affected by his troubles.

"Debbie couldn't finish her law studies and had to finish with a business school," he explained sadly. "She had to change her name to get a job in a bank."

But Mary Vincent had no education, no prospects, and no hands. None of that mattered because Debbie had to change her surname. And then Singleton really turned it on.

"I spent $27,000 on Laetrile treatments for my first wife," he said, his voice catching. "I nursed her until she died from cancer in 1977."

Legal expenses had furthered his financial decline until he was wiped out. To top everything off, he had lost his seaman's pension benefits.

"I'm contemplating filing suit in federal court," he said. *He* was the victim, Singleton maintained, a victim of kidnapping and robbery. He vowed, "When I get out of these gates, I'll have more time to work on my appeals. Right now, I'm working on the jury instructions, which were also prejudicial."

Singleton had also learned another lesson of prison life—jailhouse lawyers put the system on trial. And he would have plenty of time to do it before his parole came up in April 1987.

APRIL 1987

As Singleton's parole date approached at the end of the month, California politicians, mindful of keeping their jobs, realized they had to do something. Unless they acted, and acted quickly, Singleton would be out, and who knew what county he'd decide to settle in?

If Singleton came to *their* county, citizens would be angry, not just at Singleton, but at the politicians who had allowed him in. Come election time, those same politicians would be out. Politicians in Antioch, a northern California town near San Francisco, were the first to act.

Antioch's mayor had heard from the State Department of Corrections that there were plans afoot to parole Singleton in his town.

"Nothing doing," said Antioch's mayor, who, without much difficulty marshaled the townspeople to support his position.

Bowing to the public outcry, the Department of Corrections agreed not to release Singleton in Antioch and instead, contacted the mutilator's relatives in Tampa, Florida.

"Would you take him?" they asked.

The rationale was perfect: get Singleton out of state and he becomes someone else's problem. It was a classic case of passing the buck.

Before his family could respond, the state of Florida itself rejected Singleton. The last thing Florida wanted was Singleton violating his parole in the Sunshine State.

He was California's problem—let it stay that way.

The prevailing wisdom in the State Department Corrections was to release Singleton into Contra Costa County, where he had once lived.

On April 24, attorneys representing the Contra Costa County Board of Supervisors and four city councils within the county went into court to prevent Singleton from being released into their jurisdiction. Finding a sympathetic judge was not difficult because, in northern California, Singleton was the devil incarnate.

The attorneys easily won a temporary restraining order from a superior court judge in Martinez barring the Department of Corrections from placing Singleton anywhere in Contra Costa County. The county then turned around and served documents on Stanislaus and

San Diego counties, trying to compel *them* to take the Mad Chopper. The latter two counties would have to send their representatives to court on May 14 to argue why Singleton should not be paroled in their areas.

Singleton wasn't even out yet and he had no place to go. Corrections decided he could live in anonymity in San Francisco for two weeks after his initial release. As soon as the state told Police Chief Frank Jordan of their plans, San Francisco decided two weeks were two too many. The city had its attorneys go into Superior Court on April 24 where they, too, got a restraining order barring Singleton from entering the city limits.

The next day, April 25, Singleton caught his first breath of fresh air when he stepped outside the gates of the California Men's Colony at San Luis Obispo. He smelled the salt air from the nearby ocean, looked up at the blue sky, and then back down at the sundrenched earth. It was good to be alive, good to be *free*. He still had one little problem, though.

Lawrence Singleton wasn't sure where he would be sleeping that night, or for that matter, where he'd be sleeping any night. *Where should I go?* he wondered.

Back in Stanislaus County, the city fathers were determined to see that he stayed out of their hair. Concerned that their most notorious criminal might come back to roost, Mayor Maureen O'Connor and Police Chief William Kolender wrote a letter to state corrections officials, stating unequivocally that not only did they not want Singleton, they wouldn't accept him.

Someone like Singleton, who had committed a crime " . . . too heinous for any rational human being to comprehend, should never have been granted parole in the first place," the letter said.

Attorney General John Van de Kamp said he had sympathy for county officials who wanted to keep Singleton away from their citizens. But he characterized the situation as a "spectacle."

Steve White, the chief assistant attorney general, was probably more accurate when he added, "This has all the dimensions of a circus."

Governor George Deukmajian, a Republican who had campaigned on a hard-on-crime platform, weighed in with his feelings.

"I would personally have felt, based on what he did, he probably should have remained in prison for the rest of his life," the governor said.

But since Singleton's fourteen-year, four-month sentence was in accordance with state law, local officials had no legal right to block his parole. If that were allowed to happen in this case, Deukmajian reasoned, it could happen in any case where a county did not want to take a controversial parolee into its bosom.

"I just don't think that would be a feasible solution," the governor continued.

He pointed out that Singleton had been sentenced under California's 1977 determinate sentencing law, which gave specific terms for crimes. That law, and others the state had adopted, required that after an inmate did his time, he be released, allowing, of course, for reductions for good behavior and involvement in a work program, as in Singleton's case.

While Deukmajian supported the stricter sentencing laws that had taken effect after Singleton's conviction, and did not want a return to the determinate sentencing laws, he said, "There may be some instances where we do need to provide more flexibility for the paroling authorities . . . with respect to some individuals who have committed heinous crimes."

In other words, if a criminal like Singleton slips through the cracks in the future, we'll handle it the right way, but for now, we will just have to deal with the situation as it exists.

All this controversy put the California Department of Corrections in a quandary. They hadn't passed the sentencing laws, the state legislature—the *politicians*—had. And now those same politicians did not want to take responsibility for Singleton's release. Instead, Corrections was supposed to worry about him.

Not on your life.

Corrections appealed the restraining orders. Their position was that the counties did not have the legal authority to interfere with an inmate's parole. In private, though, no one in the department could blame the two counties. Who would want Singleton anyway? For its part, the Department of Corrections, in an effort to avoid further showdowns like this one, decided to step up their efforts to place Singleton in another state.

They tried the neighboring state of Nevada.

NOTORIOUS RAPIST SETTLES IN VEGAS

Would that be a headline good for the gambling and tourism industries that caused the state's coffers to bulge? the Nevada officials asked themselves. Of course not. No way was Singleton settling in Nevada, no way. The best part was, since he was an out-of-state resident, they didn't even have to go into court to get a restraining order. All they had to do was give a polite "no," which they did, and it was the end of their problem. For California, though, the problem was only just beginning.

Celia Johnson had read of her ex-husband's plight in paper after paper. It seemed you couldn't turn on a local newscast without seeing something about it.

She felt sorry for Larry. After all, they had shared a life together and remained friends afterward. She wondered if there was some way she could help him. Celia released a public statement that said she was willing to take him in. Singleton could live with her.

"I'm not afraid of him, and he has to live somewhere," said the compassionate nurse.

She felt that Larry deserved a chance to rehabilitate himself. Her only worry was whether her humble motor home would be the right place to start this, the latest phase in their relationship.

"It's not my right to upset this community," she said. "We'd have to find someplace else." She lived in Lake County, ninety miles north of San Francisco. "It wouldn't be safe for him here," she added.

Celia's generosity notwithstanding, the problem was not whom he'd live with, but where he'd live. Also, there might be a problem just keeping Singleton alive.

There had been anonymous threats on Singleton's life, which, given the depth of feeling against him, the state had to take seriously. Armed parole guards were brought in to shuttle Singleton to a secret location in northern California while his future residence was being sorted out.

"He's somewhere north of Bakersfield. That's all we can say," State Department of Corrections spokesman Robert Gore told the press. "We expect a very quiet weekend," he added. "We are charged with supervising a successful parole. We want a minimum of publicity."

Four days passed of what should have been his newfound freedom, but instead Singleton found himself a prisoner of his own notoriety. He was moved to a motel on Fifth Avenue in San Mateo's North Fair Oaks area. Meanwhile, the Department of Corrections was working hard to find him a home, but with little success. As soon as a community found out who it was the department wanted to place in their midst, they threatened legal action. Like San Mateo.

At first, things had been fine in San Mateo. Sheriff Arthur Baca knew Singleton was coming, that he would be temporarily paroled into his county. Baca had decided to keep the news quiet, lest a media circus be churned up by the knowledge of Singleton's whereabouts.

"This was a very temporary thing," Baca said later. "I was satisfied that there were appropriate security and supervisory measures taken by state parole," the lawman continued. "Sure, he's the type of individual that should have remained in custody. He's going to be a problem for any political jurisdiction he's released in."

That was an understatement, but there was little time to contemplate it when word leaked out of Singleton's presence. Mindful of his safety, corrections guards whisked Singleton out of town. Officials in bordering counties denied that Singleton had been foisted on them.

Back in San Mateo, Bodie Lane, president of the San Mateo County Board of Supervisors, was outraged that the state had sent Singleton to his county, even for one night.

"The whole situation has been totally shocking to me," said Lane. "There is massive opposition to this man being here."

Lane had scheduled a special meeting of the board of supervisors to block Singleton from being paroled permanently into his county.

"It may be a political sort of thing, just voicing our outrage," Lane said honestly. "It may be that all we can do is write a letter or pass a resolution."

"I got the impression that neither the board of supervisors nor the district attorney's office knew anything about it, which was kind of surprising," added Redwood City Mayor Marshal Ralston. Redwood City was another town in San Mateo County that didn't want Lawrence Singleton.

Three weeks passed, three weeks of court appearances by county officers seeking to keep Singleton out of their localities, three weeks in which the parole guards moved Singleton from location to location. For his part, Singleton was enjoying all the attention.

There was something nice, for a change, in the state doing something *for* him, rather than against him. It was as though they owed him.

He stayed in nice motels. The food was good and plentiful. He had all the smokes he needed. What could be bad?

Like Odysseus, Singleton's odyssey had to end. Eventually, the courts had to rule and they did: on May 8, the First District Court of Appeals overturned the temporary restraining orders in Contra Costa County and San Francisco, allowing state parole agents to place Singleton where they saw fit.

In other words, to heck with Contra Costa, San Francisco and all the rest of the "friendly" California localities that would not welcome Singleton into their collective bosom. The parole agents would put Lawrence Singleton where *they* wanted and there wasn't going to be any argument.

The agents decided on a motel in El Cerrito in Contra Costa County. The county fathers were infuriated, but what could they do? The appeals court had ruled and they'd lost. Maybe they would appeal to a higher court.

"I've got a better idea," said county official Claire Thomas.

Thomas had seen how averse the Department of Corrections was to publicity. After a few calls disclosed Singleton's location, the information was made public. The verbal response of the Department of Corrections was unprintable, but their physical response was immediate. Once again, Singleton was whisked out of town to an undisclosed location.

In a public statement afterward, Thomas explained her actions.

"I felt it of utmost importance to the public," to disclose Singleton's location. "It would have been inappropriate of me to withhold that information."

NINE

As Singleton struggled to find a home, Mary Vincent struggled to find a life.

While Larry cooled his heels in motel after motel, Mary Vincent continued to suffer. She gave countless interviews to magazines and newspapers about what had happened and how she was doing. There were authors who bothered her for potential books, and producers for television movies, who called her up to get the rights to her story. But no book was ever written, no movie was ever made, and Mary never made a dime off her tragedy.

She entered psychotherapy, which she continued for years. Her family split apart when her mother and father separated. Her dad went to work in Alaska, where he joined the Alaskan Air National Guard. Her mother preferred a more hospitable climate—she went to Vegas where she became a blackjack dealer. And Mary?

Mary had her prostheses all right, but no education. She did not return to school after the assault. She had not been trained for any job at the time of the assault, and she continued to be unskilled afterward.

Her total income for the ten years after the assault came from three sources. From the California Victim of Crimes Act, she got $13,000, supplemented by $6,000 in small donations from a public fund set up in her name, and finally, public assistance. Along the way, she had a relationship with a man that produced a son.

Jimmy Collins was behind the desk in the Redwood City motel when the two big guys came in. Following them was an older man who had a large, bulbous nose. The two guys came up to the front desk and asked to rent two rooms for the night.

"Together," one of the big guys added.

Jimmy looked through his room keys. It was a slow night and he had no problem finding two rooms together. The same guy who had spoken filled out the guest register and was quick to request a receipt for the money he laid out for the rooms. Maybe it was the quickness of the question or the deliberately low profile all three seemed to be trying really hard to keep that made Jimmy suspicious.

Jimmy glanced over at the guy with the nose, who turned around for a moment from the window he'd been gazing out of. It took Jimmy a second to realize who the guy was—Lawrence Singleton! But Jimmy didn't say anything. He just checked them in and gave them their room keys.

Jimmy quickly went to the phone to call an old school buddy, Saul Beltran, who was a reporter for the local paper, the *Times Tribune*. The paper told him that Saul was out on assignment. Jimmy tried again in a couple of hours, but Saul was still out.

The following morning, there was a knock at the door of Singleton's room. He opened it, figuring it was his bodyguards, only to be surprised by a flashbulb popping off in his face and a reporter firing questions at him.

"Mr. Singleton, what are you doing here? Are you settling in Redwood? How do you like—"

Singleton didn't hear anything else. By that time, his two guards had heard the commotion and came running in. They briskly packed up his things and theirs, quickly loaded them into their car, and drove off. Once more, Singleton was on the run.

They just won't leave me alone, Singleton thought. But barely had he formed that thought, when he realized that it was particularly true this time.

The *Times Tribune* staffers chased Singleton through the streets of Redwood City and into Atherton, a chase that only ended when a second Department of Corrections car blocked the street. Saul Beltran was forced to brake, and as he gazed though his windshield, he saw Singleton's car speeding into the distance.

That night, Singleton's "safe" motel was in Napa, a place that was only disclosed on a need-to-know basis. "We don't have sleazy hotels in Napa, and we want to keep it that way," said one local official who'd been asked to comment.

The new, super-secret plan now was to put Singleton in Richmond township, but once again leaks proved to be the bane of the Department of Corrections. When Bert Bevins found out that Lawrence Singleton was in town, he was furious.

Bert was a prominent Richmond businessman. The last thing he wanted was for Singleton to be around mucking up business. Who'd want to shop in a town that condoned settling the state's most famous mutilator in its midst?

After being tipped to Singleton's presence, Bevins called a news conference to focus attention on the paroled rapist, correctly anticipating Singleton's reaction. Singleton was mortified when he came home from lunch to discover camera crews camped on his doorstep. He quickly packed. The parole board needed to relocate him again. It would have been funny, had it not been so sad.

Singleton was quickly moved to the small town of Rodeo in the San Francisco Bay Area. He had now changed his name to Frank Farmer. Shortly thereafter, Minnie and Will Simpson showed up at the apartment building owned by Sybil Dahl.

"We're looking for an apartment," said Minnie.

"What did you have in mind?" Sybil asked.

"Well, it's my father—" began Will.

"He's kind of cantankerous," Minnie cut in.

"Yes, well, he doesn't have many needs. We thought a small place. He's just coming home from the hospital after a long illness," Will continued.

Sybil looked through her files. "Well, I have one studio available for $345 a month."

"We'll take it," Minnie said, sounding relieved that they had found a place for her cantankerous father-in-law.

Sybil watched as the old man was moved in by Minnie and Will. He did seem rather cantankerous, complaining at every step of the way. Sybil noticed he had a bulbous, veined nose.

Later in the day, she stopped by to formally greet him, but found two beefy guys in uniform outside his door. They seemed to be his bodyguards and they barred her from going in.

"He'll pay his rent on time, don't you worry," one of the beefy guys told her.

"But why are you here?" she asked.

He gave her some double-talk and then turned his back. That was the worst thing the guard could have done. It just made Sybil mad.

Her new resident with the large nose looked familiar. He made her feel uneasy. That brought up old feelings about her daughter Susie, who was raped and murdered in 1976.

That evening, Sybil called a friend of hers, Jerry White. Sybil and Jerry were real tight, and Jerry was one of the managers of the local TV station. She told Jerry about her new resident, and the guards outside his door. After she described the man who had moved in and under what circumstances, it was clear to Jerry who it really was.

Jerry now had a scoop. He was the only one in the state who knew where Lawrence Singleton was living. The only question that remained was how to release the news to maximum effect.

Lawrence Singleton had finally found some measure of peace. The state had rented him a furnished studio apartment. It was here, he thought, that he could finally rest.

The day after he settled in, he showed up quietly and by himself at the local sheriff's substation to fulfill the part of his parole that required him to register as a sex offender. The cop who took his report said very little, but noted his name. It was hard to miss it, since Singleton had signed it in big letters. And the cop was no dummy; he'd been watching the news for the past few weeks and knew who he was. But he was a professional. He knew of the problems Singleton had been having, and he wasn't about to add to them by disclosing his location, and getting his superiors angry at him in the bargain.

The next morning, Singleton got up, breakfasted on eggs, ham, toast, and coffee, took a long walk, and finally began to enjoy his newfound freedom. He did things that afternoon he hadn't done in years, like going to the movies, going shopping, eating at McDonald's, all the things free men and women take for granted.

He was fifty-nine years' old, with a record, but if he kept his nose clean, he might be able to live out his life in freedom. The conditions of his parole made it difficult for him to pick up women so, for a while anyway, he didn't have to worry about anyone accusing him of rape, abuse, or anything else for that matter. All in all, things were going all right.

Singleton returned home and, by midafternoon, had settled down in bed to take a nap. Soon, he was asleep.

"We interrupt your regular programming for this special bulletin."

The blond-haired reporter looked up from her notes with a gleam in her eye. Jerry had just handed her the bulletin.

"We have just received word that notorious rapist/mutilator Lawrence Singleton has taken up residence in Rodeo township. According to someone who lives in the same building as him, he has taken up residence at 1001 Elm Street, a multistory apartment house.

"Apparently," continued the reporter, "our sources tell us that Singleton was placed there by representatives of the state Department of Corrections masquerading as husband and wife. The department has refused comment. Stay tuned for further developments. We now return you to your regular programming."

The TV station was playing with fire. Given the level of public resentment against Singleton, they had just declared open season on the man. In his apartment, Singleton snoozed away, blissfully unaware of what was happening outside. His guards, playing cards, knew nothing of the broadcast, while word spread quickly of the Mad Chopper's presence within the friendly confines of Rodeo township. Reaction was swift.

The notorious rapist and mutilator had settled in among them as though he was some normal person. Townspeople wanted him out.

Some of them immediately gathered in front of his apartment house to protest.

The guards, looking down at them as they were easily dispersed by sheriff's deputies, were worried. One uttered the universal expression of concern: "Uh-oh."

That afternoon, Singleton was the topic of discussion at local bars and taverns. Rodeo was a largely blue-collar town of 7,000. Normally placid men who did their nine-to-five without complaint reacted violently.

"What the hell is he doing around here?" said one.

"Let's get rid of the son of a bitch," another offered.

Like most mobs, it started out with just a few malcontents, but pretty soon the bad vibes spread throughout the town. Women joined the ranks of the outraged. Why should they be denied the right to be part of an angry mob just because of their sex? They had as much right as anyone else to be vigilantes.

By the time Singleton awoke in the evening, his guards were on the alert for more trouble. They told him what was going on, but Singleton treated the news with little reaction. Instead, he was hungry.

Singleton pulled a TV dinner out of the freezer and warmed it up in a new gadget he had never seen before—a microwave oven. All you had to do was pop the food in, press a few buttons, and *bam*—invisible rays heated the slop up faster than anything he'd ever seen. It was amazing!

Outside, the modern-day lynch mob was gathering. Fueled by hate, they stalked down the street in search of their quarry. As they rounded the corner, they saw Singleton's apartment building.

Inside the apartment, Singleton was just finishing his meal when he heard the sounds. They were not much at first, just a few voices, but as the people got closer, he could hear that it was not just a few, but hundreds.

"Singleton out, Singleton out," they chanted.

"Kick him out, kick him out."

The guards looked down on the street to as frightening a scene as any lawman could ever hope to see. It was a mob all right, and it was clear that they were coming not to chat with Singleton, but to get him.

It was a scene lifted whole out of the late nineteenth century, when the county sheriff stood his ground as the lynch mob advanced to take away his prisoner for hanging. The difference was that Singleton had already served his time in jail and these people, unlike the law, were not satisfied with the sentence. They wanted him behind bars for life, and short of that, they wanted him out of town. If he got hurt in the process, or if manhandling him brought the man pain and suffering, who was going to complain?

Quickly, the parole agents acted, calling directly to the county sheriff's office and telling them of their plight. While they waited for help, they put Singleton in the living room, away from the window. Then they checked the ammunition clips in their automatic weapons, brought the slides back to load cartridges into the chambers, and flipped off the safeties. They made sure the door was locked, barred it, and then they waited.

Singleton was sitting in the living room, watching TV when he heard glass break in his bedroom. Someone had thrown something. While the parole agents contemplated their options, one county official, Sarah Fisher, actually showed up to see how Singleton was doing.

"It was strange," Fisher recalled later. "He seemed not to be too concerned. I think that may have been because he's been through this so many times now. The man has become a pariah. No one wants him."

"Why don't you consider serving the remaining eleven months on your parole at a minimum-security prison?" she suggested to Singleton, who turned angrily from the TV set he'd been watching, even as the mob continued to throw rocks at the windows of his apartment.

"I served my time. I'm an innocent man," Singleton reacted angrily. "Why would I go back there?"

Sirens approached from the distance. The crowd heard them and stopped as the sirens got louder and louder, and finally deafening as a phalanx of sheriff's black-and-whites pulled to the curb outside Singleton's apartment house. A group of officers went inside, while the rest stayed on the street, where they set up a police perimeter.

"Step back, please, step back," a metallic voice intoned through a police loudspeaker.

Inside there was an anxious knock at the apartment door, and when the deputies ascertained who it was, the door was swung wide open.

"Let's go," said one of the cops who'd run up the stairs.

Quickly, Singleton packed what few belongings he had managed to amass in the last month, and followed the cops out.

"Here, put this on," said one of the parole agents, who shoved a bulletproof vest into Singleton's gnarled hands.

"Stay close to us," his two parole agents advised.

When they hit the street, the crowd was contained behind the police barricades, but upon sighting Singleton, a roar went up.

"There's the son of a bitch!"

"Let's get him the hell out of here!"

"Let's have a lynching party for him."

"Hey, I've got some rope!"

"My kid plays in front of his building!"

"We want him out of here!"

Someone in the crowd was carrying a doll with its arms cut off and a sign that said THINK ABOUT IT. Someone else carried a sign that said GET OUT OF TOWN, BUD!

A mob is only as brave as its bravest man or woman. Since most mobs are composed of cowards who find strength in numbers, no one was willing to take the first step forward to go after the old man. But there was no guarantee that their nerve would continue to be low. Maybe someone would get it in his head to make a reputation by taking out Singleton.

The cops wouldn't give them the opportunity.

As sheriff's deputies moved in to disperse the crowd, the now bulletproof merchant seaman was hustled down the stairs and into a waiting squad car, which drove off, siren wailing, through the screaming throng. Before any of them realized what had happened, Singleton was gone.

There was no point in hanging around. They'd gotten what they wanted. The crowd dispersed quickly and oozed down side streets. The only things left on the sidewalk in front of Singleton's former haven were a bunch of cigarette butts and empty coffee cups that drifted down the street in the wind.

"We had a mob reaction, a mob mentality. Where does it stop?" said County Undersheriff Ward Welker.

"Let someone show me how you can legally justify mob reaction," Welker continued. "I have seen people go absolutely off the board in what they are doing and saying. This is not what our community is all about. There is a proper forum [for protest] and it is in the courts and legislative bodies."

Welker was a welcome voice of sanity in an insane situation, and the state apparently heard him. In Sacramento, the state capital, the Assembly Public Safety Committee met to consider the case of Lawrence Singleton. Was the state parole system set up to handle it? And what steps could be taken in the future to prevent the release of criminals who, like Singleton, were suspected of having mental disorders.

A 1985 law allowed authorities to commit criminals to mental institutions after their scheduled release date. According to a spokesman for the Department of Mental Health, Singleton was not kept in jail because he had not been diagnosed as having a severe enough "character disorder" to be committed.

"What I don't understand is why a man who hacks off the arms of a fifteen-year-old girl is not crazy?" questioned Assemblyman Larry Stirling (a Republican from San Diego), chairman of the Public Safety Committee.

Stirling's committee also had access to the shocking amounts of money that were being spent ferrying Singleton around Northern California. The cost alone for the Department of Corrections parole officers who had been guarding him ran to almost $4,000 a day, or nearly $30,000 a week. Of course, those figures did not include the costs for the attorneys from the state attorney general's office who were shuttling in and out of courts, four so far, to try and convince judges that Singleton had the right to be paroled—somewhere, anywhere.

"We're spending a lot of money just to carry out the law," said one high-ranking assistant attorney general. "This has all the dimensions of a circus. If all the counties in the state followed the pattern that some counties are setting, you would end up with Singleton being discharged without being on parole. Obviously, that is not going to work."

As for the Department of Corrections, they had decided that it was no longer productive to discuss the case publicly. They continued, however, to believe, despite all evidence to the contrary, that Singleton should be settled in Contra Costa County, familiar grounds to him, where he had lived before the rape and mutilation of Mary Vincent. The thought was he would be more comfortable, and less likely to violate parole, if he settled on familiar ground.

"This matter needs to be resolved so we don't go through this agony again," said Attorney General John Van de Kamp. "I have sympathy for county officials who want to keep Singleton out. It's become kind of a spectacle," he continued.

The public, though, was getting tired of the spectacle and a backlash had begun against the politicians who were fanning the fires of hate.

"Local politicians were posturing because they couldn't possibly win," said law professor John Wyant of the University of Southern California. "But what are these politicians going to say to their constituents?"

They had to show they were doing something to keep the menace out of their communities.

"Once this starts, it just tends to feed on itself," said another academic. "Politicians will do what newspapers will report. It's safe. You don't lose votes by denouncing Singleton."

In the wake of Singleton's hasty, and dangerous, withdrawal from Rodeo, Contra Costa County officials began to soften their rhetoric. While having Singleton among them would be bad for business, it would be worse if someone in the county killed him because they didn't want him there. What kind of message would *that* send?

"The snowball is so big that nobody can handle it," said county official Sarah Fisher.

She requested that the state parole authority meet with local officials to see if they could find a mutually satisfactory home for Singleton. Fisher and the rest of the Contra Costa County Board of Supervisors also met in a special closed session in an effort to resolve what had become, in the words of the media, "the Singleton problem." But two hours were apparently not enough: at the end of the meeting, no conclusion was reached.

"We are, however, prepared to work with the state to resolve the issue," Fisher said.

Meanwhile, Singleton had been placed under the jurisdiction of the neighboring community of Concord, still within Contra Costa County. Police confirmed for reporters that Singleton was at another undisclosed location, under heavy guard by four parole officers. However, he had no other police protection.

"They are telling us that Singleton will be here in Concord from two to three days," said a town official.

That night, hundreds of people gathered outside the motel where Singleton was rumored to be staying. It looked as though it might be a repeat of the scene in Rodeo. But then, an enterprising reporter found out that the whole thing was a lie.

Singleton wasn't anywhere near Concord. The parole board had spread that piece of disinformation in an effort to get everyone off Singleton's tail. Apparently, it had worked.

Singleton was somewhere, but only a few knew where that somewhere was, and for a change, no one was talking. It had become a game now, a game of hide-and-seek. Only, grownups were playing it. Where is Lawrence Singleton today?

"There's never been a case like this," said a Department of Corrections official in what was a classic bit of understatement.

TEN

TO HAVE AND TO HOLD

To Mark McCain, appearance was not as important as who the person was. And that was why, when he met Mary Vincent, he was able to immediately see the vulnerable and loving woman, and not the claws for hands. They had fallen in love.

Mark had the capacity to always make her laugh. Redheaded and twenty-three years' old, he was the boss of a landscaping crew. He had something that Mary Vincent had lacked for ten years. Mark McCain had a future, and eventually he offered to share it with her.

Now, it was the day of their wedding in a small village in the Pacific Northwest. The location had been kept a secret so that the proceedings were not inundated with prying reporters. Only three journalists had been invited, and they had all signed an agreement not to disclose the city, nor even the state where Vincent had lived for almost three years.

Mary had done a good job of covering her tracks. She didn't want Singleton, who had threatened to "finish the job," to know where she was. The Department of Motor Vehicles, a public agency, would not reveal if there was a driver's license in Mary Vincent's name, despite the fact that driver's licenses were a matter of public record. So were marriage certificates, but arrangements had been made in advance so that her marriage to Mark would not be a matter of state record.

The idea had come from Mary's attorney. By sealing public documents with her name and address, there could be no paper trail for

Singleton or anyone else to follow to the town that had taken in Mary Vincent like one of their own.

"Everyone in town kind of looks out for me to make sure I'm okay," said Mary to one of the reporters who'd signed the confidentiality agreement. It was in this mystery town which had adopted her that she felt truly safe. Residents knew of her notoriety, but wouldn't talk to outsiders about her, even when asked. They were used to minding their own business.

"It's like I was a gem that walked in here and everyone said, like, 'This girl's special, she cares a lot. So we'd better look out for her,'" was how Mary described her special relationship with the town, and it with her. "I've never had that feeling in a long time."

For the wedding, Mary looked beautiful in a white satin gown. With a minister presiding, they made their vows and Mark placed the wedding ring on Mary's hook.

As the minister pronounced them man and wife, they embraced and kissed. For Mary, it was a quiet, peaceful moment that she hoped augured well for the future.

"It [life] just began all over again," she said. "Everything that has been happening lately seems like the beginning of another life, a *better life*."

Since that awful day in the fall of 1978, Mary Vincent had been looking for peace in her world. And on her wedding day, she finally found it.

The California Gold Rush of 1849 had brought many men to northern California. Unfortunately, there were as many rogues and scoundrels and criminals among them as there were miners. Eventually, the few jails that existed at the time became overcrowded with convicted lawbreakers. Aware of the state's growing pains, the legislature knew they had to act to alleviate the situation.

There was a point extending out into San Francisco Bay, north of the city. It was land that no one wanted to build on because of its raw weather and marshy conditions. It was, therefore, the ideal place to establish a state prison—isolated, cheap, and secure. The money was appropriated for its construction.

The new prison opened its doors for the first time in 1852 and began receiving what, through contemporary times, has been a continual stream of criminals. Named for the point extending out into the bay, it was called San Quentin Prison.

While its sister prison, Alcatraz, on a small island in San Francisco Bay, catered to the worst federal offenders, San Quentin housed the most recalcitrant criminals guilty of crimes against the state. It was the place, Governor George Deukmajian felt, that posed the best solution to "the Singleton problem."

While publicly stating, "That by his barbaric acts, Lawrence Singleton forfeited his right to ever again live in civilized society," Deukmajian had grown tired of the refusal of the Northern California counties to take Singleton and what seemed like their daily efforts to get relief through the courts.

Acting to put a stop to the "circus," Deukmajian took the unprecedented step of ordering that Lawrence Singleton be housed for the length of his parole behind the walls of San Quentin prison. It was a good political move.

Deukmajian was answering his critics, who had said he had failed to act decisively as the matter snow-balled, while at the same time coming up with a solution that no one could really criticize, except perhaps civil libertarians, and who cared about them? Singleton, of course, wasn't thrilled by the prospect of going back to jail, but he didn't have much of a choice.

Under the guise of protecting Singleton from the mob and the mob from Singleton, Deukmajian's plan was to house Singleton on prison grounds under a twenty-four-hour watch of parole agents and "wherever he goes, he will be accompanied by these agents."

"With the placement of Singleton on the site of a state correctional facility, a safe distance from other communities, and with around-the-clock parole supervision, we will provide maximum public protection under the law," the governor said in his weekly radio and television address.

Deukmajian, who had a law-and-order background as a state legislator and attorney general, went on to say that, "Understandably, no community wants Singleton, and yet he must be placed somewhere." While noting that Singleton's sentence was "insufficient" despite the law in effect at his sentencing, the governor said, "I call upon all public officers and law-abiding citizens to understand that they must set a good example and that mob rule has no place in our society."

In order to prevent situations like the one they now found themselves embroiled in from reccuring in the future, Deukmajian advocated enacting a proposed constitutional amendment that would empower the governor to rescind the scheduled parole of a felon whose freedom would pose an "unreasonable threat" to public safety. He also urged that the state legislature approve a senate bill that would create the new crime of "aggravated mayhem," punishable by life without the possibility of parole.

It was an ironic solution to the problem, considering that a few days before in Rodeo, Singleton had categorically rejected Sarah Fisher's suggestion to the same effect But since then, he'd had cause to reflect, and that reflection had deteriorated into abject fear.

Between the vigilantes and the grinding travel from town to town, Singleton was scared. He knew that if he remained outside prison walls even with agents protecting him, all he could look forward to was the public continuing to hound him and the possibility that one day, soon, someone might actually follow through on the threats to kill him. When he was offered the chance to serve his time at San Quentin, he readily agreed.

On Saturday, May 30, Singleton checked into the prison at five A.M. He was immediately taken to a trailer that had been set up for his use on the prison grounds. He would be among many nonprisoners who lived at the prison—families of about one hundred prison staff members lived on the prison grounds. But their living area was made out of bounds to him, and in turn, his special housing was out of bounds to the "normal" residents.

As for company, he would have little or none. Besides the parole agents, there was no one who would come to visit him, save his ex-wife, and she couldn't come often. As for his rights, Singleton would have the same ones as any resident, subject to his parole restrictions, which were many.

Singleton was not allowed any contact with inmates, and he wouldn't be allowed to leave the immediate area where he was housed. He had to observe a curfew from ten P.M., to six A.M., but he would be allowed to leave the prison grounds, as long as his parole agents accompanied him.

In other words, he had substituted one prison for another. His trailer would be his cell until his parole was completed at the end of the year. The state would, however, help him find a job if he wanted a job in the prison, or even one outside prison walls. Singleton figured that if he could get his pension back, he wouldn't have to worry about that.

Most of the politicians who had criticized the state government for trying to place Singleton in their community praised the governor's actions.

"It's a great idea," said Sarah Fisher. "My constituents have been calling and they are very, very grateful to the governor for interceding."

"I think the governor has come up with an excellent compromise," said Claire Thomas. She felt that Deukmajian's actions effectively ended the greatest public complaint she could recall in Contra Costa County.

"It was a tremendously emotional situation," Thomas continued. "I have never in the history of this county seen anything like this."

Singleton settled into his "new" life behind prison walls. His notoriety began to fade. Other rapists took their places on the front pages, But the public, and the press, would not let him forget. Singleton was, at least for a while, determined to distance himself from the past.

For the first time since his release, he refused interview requests. Apparently, he didn't even bother to travel off prison grounds.

"Haven't see him around," said pharmacist Aaron Niles, who worked in a drugstore north of San Quentin in the town of Rafael.

"I wouldn't recognize him if I saw him," added Sally Rydell, manager of a convenience store near San Quentin.

"His picture was all over the paper for weeks. I'd recognize him if he'd been in. He hasn't," confirmed Meade Williams, a pump jockey at a gas station a mile down the road from the prison.

While admitting that "... a glitch in the law allowed him [Singleton] to get out too soon," Robert Gore, assistant director of the California Department of Corrections, said that most of Singleton's trips outside the prison were actually for weekly medical and psychological appointments at other state facilities.

Singleton definitely was out of the public eye, but the state was still very cognizant of his presence. And his crime. His parole date was coming up in April.

"When April 25, 1988, rolls around, under the law he is a free man," Gore continued. And knowing Singleton's parole date was due, politicians were starting to get riled up again about his second release.

The San Francisco deputy mayor, who'd previously commented on Singleton's case, made it known that he wanted to see the Department of Corrections have the power to indefinitely extend parole. At least that way, guys like Singleton would be on a tight leash.

"Under the present system, the criminal is eventually off parole and free to go where he wants. Our problem with that is not only a community safety problem, but a Larry Singleton safety problem," said the deputy mayor.

Dave Harkins, police chief of Twin Cities, a town in the San Quentin vicinity, was even more blunt. He indicated to the state that he would bill them for any police costs that would be incurred should Singleton's presence in his jurisdiction beget riots.

Eugene Burell, an attorney who had represented Contra Coast County in the suit that tried to block Singleton's parole in its jurisdiction, said that the parole system did not allow ample consideration of the needs of local communities.

"Parole is designed to be a system where local officials have very little input."

Burell felt that it wasn't enough to simply tell the local cops of a sex felon's presence in the community. Local elected officials should also be notified.

"How is anybody else going to make their opinion known?" Burell concluded.

Singleton, meanwhile, was thinking of a way to start a new life for himself once he got out.

Up in Oregon, farmer Tom Brennan had read of Singleton's problems and followed his case with great interest. He offered to let Singleton move in with his family and work as the farm's handyman.

APRIL 1, 1988

Singleton's parole was only weeks away when he decided to break his silence.

"I'm planning on going up to Oregon as soon as I get released," he said.

While Oregon had refused Tom Brennan's request, maybe they would allow Singleton to join a church group in an area of Oregon that he declined to name. The church group had offered to take him in. Of course, since he was going to be a free man with no constraints, he had thought about moving back to his old stomping grounds—Contra Costa County.

"I have many good law-abiding friends in Contra Costa County," Singleton told the *Antioch Daily Ledger*.

When asked how he felt about Mary Vincent, Singleton said that he was going to file a complaint against her in Placer and Marin counties. Since she'd lied about him, she should be made to answer for her behavior in court. He still maintained that the bad girl with the stick had kidnapped him.

"I am not doing this out of vindictiveness," he stated. "I'm exercising my constitutional rights."

As for what he hoped for once he was finally and truly free:

"I want the California Department of Corrections gorilla off my back."

When Mary Vincent read that Lawrence Singleton was "coming to get her," only this time legally, she was upset. Once again, her past, the past she had been trying to get rid of, would be pushed back into the spotlight.

"I think he is very dangerous and unstable. I think he's operating under a delusion [of innocence]," commented Stanislaus County District Attorney Donald Stahl. "I don't know what will happen when the pressure gets to be too much or if he falls off the wagon."

APRIL 16

"Hello?" said Lawrence Singleton when he got his party on the line.
"Yes?" said the person who answered.
"This is Lawrence Singleton."
"Why, yes, Mr. Singleton, how are you?" asked Vance Law.
"Well, I apologize for not calling sooner." And Singleton broke into tears.
"That's okay."
"I wanted to thank you again for your invitation. I'm just concerned about how my coming up there to Azalea was going to affect your church."
Law reassured him and Singleton said, "I am coming and I do want to be with you people."

The Bride of Christ Church was a fundamentalist Christian sect in Azalea, Oregon. Azalea is a small timber and mining town in rural southern Oregon. With all of three hundred residents, the town has never had any sort of infamy attached to it. At least that was what most residents thought until the invitation was tendered by Law. He had invited Singleton to come up and live with the sixty-five church members, most of whom grew their own food, raised livestock, and lived off the profits of several small businesses run by Law.

Church members dressed modestly, with women wearing below-the-knee skirts in muted colors, and scarves on their heads. Children attended a church school, and adults were paid a small salary for working on one of two farms or in church-owned cabinet shops. As for the men, they were the church leaders, while women were helpmates.

The invitation had been on the table for a while, but Singleton had finally decided to take advantage of it. "Just the fact that we want to put our heads on the line for someone the whole world wants to kill shows that we are a little different," Law told the *San Francisco Chronicle*.

"Somebody has to show this United States how to love those who have done wrong," continued Law. "If we can't do this, how are we going to show the enemies of this nation the love of Christ?"

If nothing else, it was a brave move by a man with love in his heart, trying to help someone he perceived to be a lost soul. Of course, the move backfired as soon as the public got wind of it.

Someone took a shotgun and shot up two church vehicles that, luckily, were unoccupied. The switchboard at the governor of Oregon's office lit up with 198 callers from Azalea and other Oregon communities who wanted nothing to do with the rapist/mutilator.

"The children usually wander around, but they're not going to be able to do that this summer," was a typical response from one of the area residents when he found out about Singleton's imminent arrival.

In one final effort to keep Singleton out, the town planned on having a town meeting to figure out whether they could do anything to keep Singleton from moving in with Law.

Maybe it was the fact that Azalea wasn't near the ocean, and once a sailor, always a sailor. The ocean got in your blood and you couldn't be too far from it. Or maybe it was the notoriety.

Singleton had just spent a full year in the public spotlight and the last thing he wanted—the last thing—was to be back in it again. And despite Law's good intentions that was exactly where Singleton was once again, which is why Singleton called Law to say he had changed his mind.

Law might have been disappointed, but for the rest of the tiny community of Azalea, it would be a safe understatement that the town breathed a heavy sigh of relief. That brought up the question that had been on everyone's mind the previous April when Singleton was paroled: where was Lawrence Singleton now? He was out, finally, and people were worried. Newspapers speculated, callers to radio programs offered Singleton "sightings," until finally, word came through that Singleton was living in Berkeley.

Singleton had a tough time finding a place to live. Every time he called landlords, when they heard his name, they slammed down the phone. Singleton was exasperated and couldn't figure out why they wouldn't talk to him. But this wasn't Lawrence Singleton: it was *Larry Ellis* Singleton.

A thirty-eight-year-old man who had been on a five-year trip around the world in 1978, he knew nothing of the assault on Mary Vincent until a friend sent him a newspaper clipping. After reading it, he forgot all about the case until Singleton's parole. That was when the two got confused in the public's mind and the law-abiding Singleton was suffering.

Besides the landlord difficulties, he had been the brunt of numerous wisecracks and cruel jokes. He had considered changing his name, but decided that was too drastic. He just hoped that the "bad" Singleton would stay out of the Bay Area and that eventually, the name "Singleton" would fade from the headlines as it once had.

Since the Singleton sighting in Berkeley had been wrong, he had to be some place, but where? Radio talk-show hosts kept the topic front and center and why not? It was great for ratings.

In late June, Singleton wrote a Southern California court that he was living in northern California, in the town of Richmond. This came as a surprise to the people of Richmond. Police officers in the town said he was nowhere about. The address he'd used in the letter turned out to be a state parole office, where his former parole supervisor worked.

"I haven't seen him since the day he was off parole," said the former supervisor. He had not registered in Richmond as a sex offender either.

While he was missing from the public eye, Mary Vincent had gone to court and gotten a 2.4 million-dollar judgment against him. "The reason he did not show up in court is he was probably afraid of being shot," Mark Edwards, Vincent's attorney, told reporters. "I can tell you we don't want him shot. We want him alive, healthy, and employed, and making payments."

Fat chance. At the age of sixty, Singleton wasn't about to go to sea again. And if he didn't do that, he wasn't trained for anything else.

Mary would have to be satisfied with whatever paltry sum her lawyers could exact from Singleton's hide.

Lawrence Singleton was weary. There was no place to go where he wouldn't be hounded. He felt like a child, alone and afraid. Where could he go for safety and security?

What does a child do when he's in trouble?

Go home. The safety and security of home. And Singleton, who had regressed to this childlike state, decided that was exactly what he'd do. Having no place to turn, he went back to where he came from.

In June, his former parole supervisor received a call from Singleton.

"Hi, I'm in Florida," Singleton said over the phone. "I'm living with my brother in the Forest Hills neighborhood of Tampa."

Then he gave his address, even though he wasn't required by law to do so. The parole officer figured that Singleton had read about the Singleton sightings in California and called to set the record straight. After exchanging pleasantries, Singleton hung up.

Now, finally, California had what it had originally wanted—Singleton was no longer its problem. He was off parole and back home where he belonged. As far as California was concerned he could live anywhere, just as long as it wasn't in their state.

For its part, Florida could do nothing to keep Singleton out. He had served his time. He was free to travel and live anywhere he wanted. But, according to Florida law, as well as the conditions of his parole, he did have to register as a convicted felon, which he initially failed to do when he relocated.

This gave Florida its out if they decided to use it. They could press charges against him for failing to register, but what was really the point? Failing to register was a misdemeanor, punishable by a minimum sentence, and then he was out on the street. The courts were already overtaxed with really serious offenses.

Singleton did eventually register as a convicted felon. As he had told his California parole officer, he was living with his brother Walter Singleton in Tampa. He had no plans to move to Oregon or anywhere else. He would stay in Florida. He had applied for his Florida driver's license using Walter's address.

As far as the cops were concerned, that made the whole matter moot. Maybe Singleton would just settle down in Tampa and live out his life in anonymity. But the public had not been reckoned with.

"We want him the hell out."

"We don't want that type of individual living here."

"We're concerned about the young girls living in our neighborhood."

These were just some of the milder comments on the call-in radio programs. The police tried to reassure the public. But the bottom line was, the police had no control over the situation.

Lawrence Singleton was back home for good, and there wasn't a damn thing anyone could do about it.

ELEVEN

Ever since the assault on Mary Vincent eleven years before, Singleton's family had lived under a self-imposed, media blackout. That didn't change when he moved back to Tampa.

Repeated attempts by reporters to contact his family for a statement about their notorious sibling failed. None of his seven brothers and sisters would talk. But amongst themselves, it was a different story.

They were a good and close family, presented with a crisis that no families had ever had to tackle. One of their own had done the unthinkable: cut off a girl's hands. They were repelled by what he had done, but united in their desire to help him. He was their brother and he needed to be taken care of now that he was home.

For his first few years in Tampa, he alternated living in his brother's and sister's homes. Newspaper reports at the time show that when vigilantes discovered he was living at his sister's, someone took some BB shots at the house. Some younger Floridians, interested in publicizing the state's citrus crop, lobbed oranges instead.

The Singleton family eventually reached a decision to rent him an apartment in the Tampa area. The town they chose, twenty miles outside the city limits was Gibsonton.

As Lawrence Singleton was driven by his family to his new home, he looked out and saw a bridge rising in the distance. Soon, they were on the bridge that spanned the Alafia River just south of Tampa.

On the other side, a sign at the bottom of the bridge said GIBSONTON. Looking around, Singleton saw marshland dotted with trailers here and there. Coming up on his immediate right was a series of low-lying buildings, what looked like a restaurant, and a trailer park. The sign at the entrance read GIANT'S CAMP. It was that, literally.

When the world's tallest man, eight-foot-six-inch Al Tomaini and his wife, Jeanie, "The World's Only Living Half Girl"—Jeanie was born with the lower half of her body missing—decided to quit the carnival, they set up the combination restaurant-and-trailer park they called "Giant's Camp" to make their living from.

Gibsonton was the place where carnival people came to winter during the off-season, and eventually retire after their performing days were over. Many of them were sideshow attractions like Jeanie and Al. It was in Gibsonton where the world-famous "Lobster Boy," Grady Stiles, Jr., lived and his buddy "Midget Man," Harry Glenn Newman, Jr. The "Bearded Lady" lived here and so did "Crocodile Man."

In despair, the Singleton family had turned to the one place on earth where their freak of a brother could live in peace, for Gibsonton was a town of freaks. The only difference was that the other residents had genetic disabilities that made them look outwardly bizarre, but for the most part, they were good people.

Lawrence Singleton was a freak on the inside, whose personal demons tore at him, hungering to escape. When they were unleashed by alcohol, he became bizarrely violent. In Gibsonton, though, he could live in anonymity. And because of his outward normality, he could live in a place where he'd feel superior.

Singleton took up residence in a cottage behind the home of Fred Loerke. Loerke, in his late seventies, formed an immediate bond with the younger Singleton, then in his early sixties. In Loerke's presence, Singleton finally found some measure of peace.

The two older men spent hours and hours talking about life and love and their adventures as young men. They spent evenings bowling at the local bowling alley. What was good for Singleton and all those around him was that when he was with Loerke, Singleton drank very little, because Loerke was a teetotaler. Singleton didn't give up alcohol completely, though. He couldn't. He was an alcoholic, and since he failed to admit that and seek help from Alcoholics Anonymous or some other organization, he continued to drink. Alone.

On many a night, you could probably find Singleton drinking in Showtown, USA. Showtown was the local watering hole where the carnies liked to hang out and shoot the breeze. Singleton was at the bar, drinking one night when he saw something that even to his eyes looked strange.

A man came into the bar, walking as quickly on his hands as he might have if they had been feet. But he didn't have feet, save for appendages that looked like an elf's slippers, with one toe curled up at each end. He walked on his hands, but they were not hands really, more like claws. A genetic defect had left his fingers fused in the shape of lobster claws.

"Gimme my usual," said Lobster Boy to the bartender as he smoothly climbed on top of a stool and pulled a wad of bills out from his pocket. Still staring, Singleton could only marvel at the dexterity of those claws.

"How ya doin? I'm Grady Stiles," said Lobster Boy, extending a claw.

"Pretty good," said Singleton, extending his hand and shaking the claw, which was as rough and as hard as a piece of oak. "My name is Bill Johnson."

Singleton was using that name so no one would know who he really was. He had found through bitter experience that his notoriety followed him around. Ironically, that had been the name of the one-armed man in the TV drama, *The Fugitive*.

The two men chatted for a bit. Yes, sir, this was a place where Singleton could feel right at home. He could drink here and no one would give him a second look.

Many addicts like Singleton have other medical problems. In Singleton's case, he would later be diagnosed as suffering from depression, paranoia, and schizophrenia that all remained untreated. That was the purpose of the alcohol—to suppress the other diseases so he could survive.

The problem is that alcohol does not solve the underlying problems that remain to eat away at the addict's conscience, if he has one. Singleton did. He desperately wanted help, but didn't know how to get it. In his mind, he formed the subconscious idea that stealing might be the way to go.

On April 8, 1990, Lawrence Singleton entered a drugstore in the town of Brandon and stole a ten-dollar disposable camera. Conveniently, he allowed himself to get caught.

Local members of the New York vigilante group, the Guardian Angels, picketed the courthouse when he was charged. Tried and convicted, he served sixty days of a six-month sentence for the theft. Six weeks after his release, on November 23, Singleton walked into a Wal-Mart in Plant City and stole a three-dollar hat.

"I just want to plead 'no contest' with an explanation," Singleton told Hillsborough Judge James Dominguez. "I'm a confused, bungle-headed old man." He explained to the judge that he was caring for a seventy-five-year-old man (probably Loerke), and had gone to Wal-Mart to buy adult diapers.

"I picked up the hat to buy for my friend," he told the judge, "paid for the diapers and just forgot to pay for the hat."

Security officers spotted the theft and followed him outside, where they nabbed him. He had no identification on him and gave his name as Bill Johnson.

"Whether or not he's crazy and has the propensity to steal, I don't know," said the assistant state attorney prosecuting the case. "I just think he's stupid. He's a thief."

Noting Singleton's California record, and the conviction on the previous shoplifting charge, the prosecutor asked for the maximum sentence under law: two years for petty theft and giving a false identity.

Singleton was soon convicted. More than fifty people packed the courtroom and applauded when he was sentenced to two years in the Hillsborough County Jail.

A two-year stretch in a minimum security jail was nothing to a man who had done almost eight in San Quentin, nine if you counted his parole year. When he got out, he went back to live with his friend Fred Loerke. But Loerke was ill, suffering from cancer. Suddenly, Singleton had to confront the reality that his only friend might die. And he would be alone.

1994

Nancy Glass, the host of the popular, syndicated tabloid show *American Journal*, looked out from the TV screen and introduced the next segment. It was, she said, about a woman whose arms had been cut off in a savage attack in 1978. The screen suddenly lit up with the face of Mary Vincent. Then, the camera panned down to show her hooks.

"He took away my pride, my esteem, my childhood," said Mary.

In the graphic, tearful interview that followed, Mary said, "I mean, this isn't living, this is existing." She told *American Journal* that she lived in hiding, in fear of her attacker, Lawrence Singleton, who remained free on parole somewhere in Florida. She would not identify the city where she lived, but she said that because of her continued upset over the attack, she had considered suicide.

"I'm haunted when I wake up. I'm haunted when I'm sleeping," she said in the interview. "It won't leave, it's always there.

"As I get older, it's getting harder to use my arms, and I have to keep myself in shape just to deal with the everyday chores, the everyday life.

"I have to work ten times harder than the average person with hands to do anything, fold clothes, do dishes," Mary continued.

She revealed on the show that she and Mark had divorced, after they had had a son together. Clearly, her life after marriage had not turned out the way she had hoped.

In 1996, Singleton's best friend, Fred Loerke, died from cancer. Singleton was bereft—he had lost his one friend in all the world and didn't know what to do. He was sixty-eight years old, and everyone was hounding him. They all wanted to frame him, to put him away. Why couldn't they just leave him alone?

He continued to try to drink away his troubles, to no avail, and he went on drunken binges. Singleton regularly patronized whores, sometimes two at a time. Once, he had a mother and her daughter, the latter following in the family tradition.

His continued aberrant behavior finally caused some family members to throw up their hands in disgust and frustration. They just didn't know what to do with him. Herb, the brother who was in business in Atlanta, took charge and decided it was time for Lawrence to move and to settle down in his own home. The hope was that this would give him the grounding he had lacked since his conviction in California.

In July 1996, a man calling himself "Bill Singleton" put a $10,000 down payment on a converted ex-Army barrack in the Orient Park neighborhood of Tampa. He agreed to pay the owner another $15,000 over the next few months to make the full purchase price. It was money that his brother Herb had given him. And that was how Lawrence Singleton, using another alias, became a property owner again. The house needed work and Singleton had all the manpower he needed in his family.

"His brothers Herb, Walter, and Jimmy would come over and josh each other while they redid the front of the house. He put in irrigation pipes so big [that] his brothers laughed at the size of them. Bill just wanted to make sure they did the job. It was a real tight family," recalls one neighbor.

Singleton became friendly with his neighbor and revealed a telling detail about his life. "The only thing he said about his mother was she drank a lot," the same neighbor recalled.

Whether it is a genetic defect, something learned in the home or a combination of both, alcoholism is looked on as a disease. It frequently runs in families. In Singleton's case, the apple had apparently not fallen far from the tree.

Despite this problem, by all accounts, he was a good neighbor.

"He was a *great* neighbor. He would come over with steaks for the barbecue. I had a rottweiler and he begged me to sell it to him," the neighbor said.

Singleton, always a dog fancier, finally convinced his neighbor to sell him the dog, which he named Kayla. But the demons were working their destruction on his insides. "He was always talking about whores. He said he had been married twice and that one of his ex's was an attorney. He had had a girlfriend who was married and taking him for all he was worth. They broke it off at Christmas. He had a real intimacy problem."

Singleton knew no matter how many women he had at a time, no matter how much he drank, he would always be left with himself. He was a man who had cut off a girl's arms, a lonely, old man whom he hated more than anything in the world. Maybe it was time to check out.

FEBRUARY 1, 1997

It was a bright, sunny day, the temperature hovering around eighty, without a cloud in the sky. The air was dry with not a trace of humidity.

Lawrence Singleton went down to his local Sears, where he "boosted" an eighty-seven-dollar power drill. After he was charged with shoplifting, he was released and sent home. When he got there, he sat down at his dining room table and wrote out a note that said simply:

> I would like to thank everyone who helped me, especially
> Herb. I hope I can find peace.

He left the note on the dining room table and went outside. His van was already in the driveway, where he'd parked it earlier in the day.

Across the street, his neighbor Stu Simon watched as he took a length of hose from his garage, and attached it to the tail pipe. Then he pulled the hose around and stuck it through the top of the driver's side window, which was open just a crack. Singleton opened the door, got in, and started the car up.

My God, he's trying to kill himself, Simon thought. Simon ran across the street, threw the car door open, and pulled Singleton out.

THE MAD CHOPPER

"What are you crazy, Mr. Bill?" asked Simon.

Simon thought that Singleton should go to the hospital to get some help. He knew the man had psychiatric problems. It was no secret. Everyone in the neighborhood knew. But trying to kill himself in broad daylight, that was just plain nuts.

Singleton declined help and went inside his house. An hour later, Stu saw him come out and try the same thing again. As before, Stu pulled him out. Once again, Singleton went back into his house.

Stu was inside his own house the next time it happened, but when he came out, he saw Singleton slumped unconscious behind the wheel of his van. He pulled him out and this time, Singleton couldn't refuse help when the police came.

Immediately, he was taken to an area psychiatric hospital. Examined by psychiatrists, they concluded that Singleton should be locked up before he hurt himself or anyone else.

"He is incapable of surviving alone or with the help of willing and responsible family or friends," the doctors wrote," (and) all available restrictive alternatives . . . have been judged to be inappropriate. . . . There is substantial likelihood that in the near future, he will inflict serious harm on himself or another person."

Their opinion was prepared as part of a report intended to help commit Singleton for long-term psychiatric care. His family pleaded with the doctors to keep him in custody. But after being put on medication, he was inexplicably released three days before a scheduled commitment hearing.

Singleton went back to spending time at the Brandon Crossroads bowling alley, about five miles from his home. A decent bowler, he had trouble getting matches because of his notoriety. Players in the Thursday and Monday afternoon leagues had already refused to play on his four-man team. The Tuesday night bowling league protested his very presence on the alleys.

Singleton felt alone, ashamed, and despised. But he wasn't the only one.

TWELVE

FEBRUARY 9, 1997

East Hillsborough Boulevard runs through Orient Park. It is a desolate, sunburned landscape where the air reeks of stale French fries from the fast food chains and gasoline from filling stations that dot the washed-out street.

The ten blocks between Fortieth and Fiftieth Streets on Hillsborough are pockmarked with by-the-hour motels and down-at-the-heels businesses that crowd for space with passing trucks that spew their dirty exhaust. Even the occasional palm tree set off to the side on a neat median of indestructible grass cannot offer the scene anything less than unrelenting gloom.

This was one of the many strips in the city frequented by whores, who liked to approach the men in the cars that floated by on their way to wherever, and propose simple business transactions that involved sex for money. Sometimes, the street would get so crowded, there'd be fifteen cars backed up on Fiftieth Street, with the prostitutes sticking their heads in the johns' cars, and other places, hustling for business.

Roxanne "Roxie" Hayes was one of the most popular women who worked the streets. Maybe it was her size. At six feet and 170 pounds, Roxie really stood out. Well-built and friendly, she was one of the johns' favorites.

While the buses had long since stopped running on the boulevard, the benches were still there, and one of them belonged to Roxie. Well, it didn't really belong to her exactly, but Roxie had been there for so long that everybody thought of it as hers, even the cops.

Deidre Lawrence, who worked in the county sheriff's office, used to see her on the same bench on her way to and from work.

"I saw Roxie today on her bench," Deidre would tell the vice guys when she got to work. Deidre worked at the county jail, Roxanne's sometime residence.

Roxie had shown up there for booking one-hundred times from 1992 to 1997. Because Deidre took East Hillsborough to work, she saw Roxie every day. A few times, she was tempted to stop and speak with her—the girl looked as though she could do better for herself, but Deidre wasn't a social worker and, besides, she couldn't be late for work. So she'd pass Roxie and wonder what she was doing there.

What Roxie was doing there was business, pure and simple, capitalism with a capital "C." It was her bench and Roxie was as polite as could be about it. The woman spent a lot of time on that bench, waiting for clients, which gave her time to think.

Roxie, thirty-two, thought a lot about her kids. There was Xena, a shy, polite girl, an honor student with plans to earn a scholarship to private school. Xena was hers by a previous relationship.

For the last few years, she had lived with Fred Ricker, and though their relationship had never been legally formalized, she thought of him as her husband, so much so that she bore him two boys, aged seven and three.

Sitting out on that bench under the hot Florida sun, inhaling the noxious exhaust fumes of East Hills-borough Boulevard, Roxie thought how her life had changed after she met Ricker on this very street.

"Can you give me a ride?" Roxie had asked him, poking her head through the open front window to where Ricker sat behind the wheel.

So he gave her a lift. Roxie slept in his car, they talked about her daughter, and then, he drove her to his sister's house. She slept there for a couple of days and from that point onward, the relationship blossomed.

Roxie remembered having their first son in 1989. She had been serving a jail sentence on a prostitution charge when her water broke and she went into labor. After she gave birth, a Hillsborough County sheriff's deputy shackled her to her bed in the hospital maternity ward.

Things were just slightly better when her second son was born four years later, in 1993. She was under house arrest at the time on some sort of drug beef, and her first call was to her probation officer, because she couldn't go anywhere, including the hospital, without his permission.

Looking out at the traffic on East Hillsborough, waiting for her next trick to show up so she could pay her rent, Roxie thought of what had happened afterward.

From bad to worse, bad to worse, that was how her life had gone. Ricker had been working as a trucker but he injured himself in a car accident in July 1996. He needed surgery on his left knee and was forced to use a wooden cane to get around. He had not worked in the intervening time, which just put that much more pressure on Roxie to be the family's principal breadwinner.

Like any dutiful husband taking his wife to work, Ricker would frequently drive his wife, leaving her at the bus stop to do her business, while going home to take care of the kids. She wanted what all parents want, what was best for her children, and she was determined to give it to them. At least that was how she rationalized it. To her, prostitution was just a business. She only fucked men for money to meet expenses.

The truth was, there was another reason that Roxanne Hayes worked as a prostitute: she was a cocaine addict and needed the money to support her habit. She had been an addict for years. Her two youngest had been lucky they had not been born addicted to the drug.

Her musings were interrupted when a white van pulled over from the traffic and stopped at the curb. Roxie went over and stuck her head in to talk to the driver.

She knew this guy. His name was Bill. They had been together twice before. Boy, was he an ugly cuss, she thought. His face had more lines than a map of China. His bulbous nose stood out like a great big wart. It was the nose of a drunk, what with the broken blood vessels, an assumption borne out by his ruddy complexion and the smell of booze on him.

Roxie negotiated. He was a john, after all, and it wasn't important how a john looked, but how much he'd pay.

"Why don't you come over to my house?" Bill asked. "I live right around here."

The two previous times they'd been together, he'd been okay. The guy didn't look particularly dangerous and besides, it'd be better inside than out; no chance of a cop catching them in a parking lot somewhere. Roxie agreed, got in, and the john took off. She looked back at the bench as she drove away.

A few hours later, Gene Reynolds, a painter who had recently painted Singleton's house, came by to do some touch-up work. He knocked on the door, and when no one answered, peered through the living room window to see if anyone was home.

He saw Singleton. It looked like he was punching a girl repeatedly in the chest. She looked in bad shape. He ran to call 911.

Singleton had just put on his condom when the disagreement started. Mindful of the increased street price of cocaine, and therefore of the increased price of her habit, Roxie asked for more money. Singleton refused, and they argued. He'd been drinking.

Anger and booze. It was as deadly a combination as any drug imaginable. Singleton's rage boiled to the surface and when it got there, it spouted out like lava from a volcano.

Singleton went into the kitchen and came back with a knife. Roxie screamed, but no one heard her. Singleton grabbed her and the murder started.

What Reynolds thought was punching was actually stabbing. Over and over, Lawrence Singleton plunged a knife into Roxanne Hayes's body. When he did, he saw everyone who had ever hated him, everyone from that girl back in Modesto to those idiots down at the bowling alley who wouldn't let him bowl with them.

When he had finished, both he and the girl were covered with blood. She managed to crawl away from him and onto his couch.

"Hold me," she implored, as her life's blood seeped out of her body. "Hold me," she whispered.

The rage had dissipated. Singleton dropped the knife and went over and took the woman he had murdered in his arms and slowly, he rocked her like a father would his child.

PART THREE
RETRIBUTION

THIRTEEN

A police search of Singleton's house turned up a bloody knife that police surmised was the murder weapon. That would be confirmed after forensic testing. By that time, Singleton was already downtown and talking to reporters who had followed him after his booking.

"I did it, I did it," Singleton shouted at reporters. "The first time was a frame, but this time, I did it."

He delivered those comments to a waiting and willing camera crew from a local TV station, that promptly broadcast them, over and over and over. Singleton was determined to end his suffering one way or another, and if it took a confession on TV to get his ass into the electric chair, so be it.

The news of Singleton's arrest for the murder of Roxanne Hayes immediately went out over the wires. Reaction was instantaneous.

"Between his past and his trying to commit suicide, I thought it was just a matter of time before something like this happened," said a neighbor.

"Gee, what a surprise," said Richard Breshears, now a captain of police.

"I'm not surprised by it," said retired Stanislaus County District Attorney Donald Stahl. "He's been disintegrating all his life."

"I have the utmost compassion for the victim and the victim's family," said former Contra Costa County executive Sarah Fisher. "I'm proud that our community rallied together to keep him out."

"It's a sad commentary on our criminal justice system that a person of this notoriety who has committed a crime this heinous is out on the streets," said a spokesman for the Hillsborough County Florida Sheriff's office, clearly shifting the blame to California for letting Singleton out of prison in the first place. But in California, Governor Pete Wilson, a conservative Republican, was not going to pass the buck. "This man deserved to be locked away forever. The law should never, ever have allowed his release from prison. He was clearly dangerous. I think he is an animal."

Wilson was tough enough to admit that California bore some responsibility for Singleton's crimes, while reiterating the problem with the state sentencing laws at the time of the mutilation.

"The law was inexcusably lenient, absurdly lenient, and now some poor woman in Florida has paid for it. It made no sense to allow someone who is as dangerous as Singleton to be released because he'd done a good job folding shirts in the prison laundry."

Under present California law, Wilson noted, Singleton would have gotten at least twenty-five years in prison for his crimes. He would have been prosecuted under the "one strike" law, which the California Legislature passed in 1994. But that was all twenty-twenty hindsight. With it, Roxanne Hayes was alive. Without it, she was on the slab in the coroner's office.

The next day, Singleton was led into the courtroom for his formal arraignment. He was wearing an orange jail jumpsuit, similar to the one he had worn nineteen years before during his first arraignment in Modesto. It looked as though there were the same chains around his wrists and ankles.

"Mr. Singleton, I need to ask you a few questions," said State Supreme Court Judge Bob Mitcham.

Singleton stood at the defense table. At his side was public defender John Skye. Across from them at the prosecution table sat Assistant State's Attorney Lyann Goudie.

The judge looked down at his file.

"Mr. Singleton, do you receive four hundred dollars a month in social security?" the judge asked.

"Yes, sir," Singleton responded.

"And all you have is five hundred dollars in assets?"

"Yes, Your Honor."

Which meant the defendant was indigent and qualified for a public defender.

After the court clerk read the charges, the judge asked, "Mr. Singleton, how do you plead?"

"The defendant pleads not guilty to all charges," public defender John Skye answered for him.

"Upon conviction, the prosecution intends to seek the death penalty," stated Assistant State's Attorney Goudie.

In light of the seriousness of the charges and the defendant's previous record, the prosecution then asked that Singleton be held without bail. That left Skye with few options.

He could oppose the motion, but what was the point? Bail was rarely, if ever, given in a capital case. Even if it had been, Singleton had no money to meet it.

The judge banged down his gavel. "So ordered," he said, and Singleton was held without bail, and taken back into a holding cell while the lawyers and judge conferred at the bench. March 18 was the date set to argue a motion for the release of records from St. Joseph's Hospital Psychiatric Care Center, where Singleton had been taken after his suicide attempt weeks before the murder.

The wheels of justice turn slowly and it was anticipated by all parties concerned that it would take a full year of pretrial motions, psychiatric evaluations, and the like before the case came to trial. In the meanwhile, Singleton had three squares a day, proper medical attention, and a clean, dry place to sleep at night, with color TV—that admittedly, he did have to share with his fellow inmates.

Singleton's incarceration made headlines, first in south Florida, and then across the country. Much attention was focused on why he had been allowed out on bail to begin with. Pundits in California and

Florida, on CNN and local stations, questioned how Singleton had slipped through the cracks in the system.

The country's mood seemed to be one of retribution and the media reflected that. No one talked about the man's psychomedical problems, which had been untreated for most of his lifetime, or his combat in Korea, which might have started, and/or exacerbated what already existed.

One angle reporters did take was the most obvious one: seek out his other victim. Get some sound bites and great shots. Which was how Mary Vincent came to be back in the news.

Reporters found Mary living in Tacoma, Washington. It was to Tacoma that she had moved after the assault, and right before her marriage. Long divorced from Mark McCain, she was raising her two children alone. She reflected on what had happened to her.

"When I start thinking about things, like how raw my arms are, I start thinking I'm not useful anymore. That's why I think about my kids and how beautiful they are."

The prosthetic arms she wore were old and broken, the cables holding them in place snapped and frayed. Because of their poor condition, they rubbed her skin red and raw, and their weight alone gave her backaches. But she was poor, almost destitute, and couldn't afford new ones, which cost $18,000 to $20,000 a pair. She had been devastated to hear of Singleton's murder of Roxanne Hayes. "I'm distraught. For the last three days"—since she had heard about the crime—"I've lost all sense of time. I haven't been able to eat, I haven't been able to sleep."

The memories of the 1978 assault had returned, stronger and more powerful than ever. She recalled Singleton's warning after the assault.

"I'm going to finish the job someday."

"My kids are the reason why I'm still alive," she continued. "I'm struggling, I'm really struggling, but you can't stop being a mother."

There might, however, have been a ray of sunshine, with Singleton again in the spotlight and the news media seeking her out. Mary had decided to try to sell her story and had contacted an agent. The idea was that any money brought in could be used to help set up a trust fund for her and her two sons.

Actually, had Singleton been a wealthy man, she would have been a wealthy woman. The civil court jury years before had awarded her a judgment of over two million dollars against him. Unfortunately, his law bills had left him practically broke and she collected almost nothing. When the judgment failed to generate any appreciable assets, Mary was forced to file for bankruptcy. She was subsequently thrown off welfare and lost her home.

"I was just starting to get happy again," she recalled. "It's been a really slow process. But I was starting to feel those little glimpses of happiness again."

Of her assailant, she characterized him as "nothing but pure evil." She couldn't understand why Singleton hadn't been locked up forever. "I've already seen what he can do with me," Vincent said.

Amazingly, she claimed not to have felt any anger over the attack on her. "Right now, I'm still stunned, and very disappointed and horrified."

DECEMBER 1997

In Florida, cameras are allowed into the courtroom. Those in support of the first amendment say that cameras promote free speech. Those against cameras, say they trample on the rights of the accused. In the Singleton case, the camera initially worked against the system.

The jury pool had been narrowed to forty-eight prospective jurors when Francine Leiter, who was part of that forty-eight, arrived home from court. She turned on the TV and was surprised to see herself. The courtroom camera had inadvertently captured her sitting in the jury box. This violated the anonymity of juries that is so important to the system's functioning effectively.

The next day, Francine complained to Judge Mitcham that her anonymity had been compromised. Judge Mitcham immediately declared a mistrial. He said that the jury process was tainted because the media had violated his order not to broadcast closeups of prospective jurors.

Mitcham reprimanded the media and then dismissed the jury. Retrial was set for February.

Two months passed. Since the trial in December, there had been changes in the jury selection process that Judge Mitcham hoped would provide a larger and more varied jury pool to choose from.

Back in December, the jurors had been pulled from voter registration rolls, the usual way it was done in most states, and in Florida as well. But under a new law that went into effect on January 1, 1998, jurors would now be culled from a pool of licensed drivers. It made sense.

As far as the jury pool was concerned, the only way the new law could work against the prosecution was if the jurors eventually picked were sympathetic to Singleton. Considering the extensive pretrial publicity surrounding the case, including persistent rehash of the California mutilation of fifteen-year-old Mary Vincent, finding a jury that had never heard of the case, or was sympathetic to Singleton was extremely unlikely.

The public defender had a snowball's chance in hell of getting Singleton off. Never mind that he had committed the murder and they were prepared to admit that at trial, though the prosecution did not know that at the time. If they had, it still wouldn't have made any difference. State's Attorney Harry Coe had always intended to argue for the death penalty.

The best the public defender could hope for was a jury that was at least willing to hear their case, have a little mercy, convict on second-degree murder and spare Singleton from the death chamber.

FEBRUARY 1998

It didn't take long for the lawyers and judge to select a jury. They did it in one day of voir dire or questioning of jurors, on Friday, February 13. Mitcham wound up seating an eleven-man, three-woman panel that included two alternate jurors.

The jury was finally seated at the end of the day. "Opening arguments to begin Monday, February 16," said Mitcham. The lawyers were left the weekend for final preparation.

Because of the intense local publicity surrounding the case, Judge Mitcham decided to sequester the jury at a downtown hotel. He also ordered that stories about Singleton be removed from their morning newspapers. He even made their drivers responsible, telling the taxi drivers who would transport them to and from the hotel to keep their mouths shut about the case.

All good and well, of course, and laudable to try and keep the jury's mind clear. But Mitcham could not be there when jurors turned on the TV or radio. He could not be there to monitor them when TV reports came on with coverage of the trial, the quotes from the prosecutors and public defenders that would accompany most of the reportage, or the sound bites that Tampa's all-news radio stations would use to lead their coverage. Jurors would be on their honor to turn the TV to another channel or the sound off the radio.

MONDAY, FEBRUARY 16, 1998

The trial of Lawrence Singleton on the single count of murder in the first degree against Roxanne Hayes opened on a sunny, brisk day, the kind of winter day that Floridians treasure. Prosecutors Jay Pruner and Michelle Peden represented the state; public defenders John Skye and Jill Menadier stood for the defense.

Pretrial motions prevented the prosecution from bringing in the mutilation of Mary Vincent. That would prejudice the jury. However, during the sentencing phase—if Singleton was convicted on murder one, there would be a separate sentencing phase—then, they could introduce the mutilation history.

Prosecutor Michelle Peden began the day's proceedings with a stinging opening argument labeling Singleton a cold and calculating murderer, who killed Roxanne Hayes in one single, cold, premeditated act.

Concerned that jurors might be sympathetic to Singleton because of his age, she brought attention to his weathered countenance. "The defendant might look like an uncle, a grandfather, a neighbor, somebody you sit next to at a baseball game, but looks can be quite deceiving. He very brutally and violently murdered Roxanne Hayes."

She made it a point to say that Singleton had already confessed to the crime, to a paramedic who arrived on the scene to treat Hayes, who unfortunately had already expired because of Singleton's actions. She outlined the evidence against Singleton that her side would present and confidently predicted that at the end, when the jurors heard everything, they would readily come back with a guilty verdict.

For the defense, the case was not so black and white. Much gray existed and if Assistant Public Defender Jill Menadier could prove that to the jury, she would save Lawrence Singleton's life.

"It was a spontaneous eruption of emotion," Menadier told the jury in her opening statement. "There was no premeditation. Larry Singleton never thought about it, never considered killing Roxanne Hayes."

In the scenario the defense lawyer painted, the day of the murder went something like this:

On February 19, 1997, Singleton, recently released from a psychiatric facility, was depressed. He was also drunk as a skunk. That, plus the medication he was taking for his psychiatric condition, considerably addled his mind. Desperate for female companionship, he found Roxie at her regular bench, and picked her up.

Singleton fancied himself a gentleman; he wouldn't have sex before dinner. So he cooked her dinner, and then they had consensual sex. But things did not go well. Roxanne decided that the agreed-upon amount for sex and for a cab ride back to Hillsborough Avenue or her home, whichever she chose, was just not enough.

"She's upset because the price of her cocaine had gone up and she needs to make money," Menadier told the jury.

She became "agitated" and demanded more money. An argument ensued and Hayes grabbed Singleton's wallet to get the money she felt he owed her. They began to struggle. She grabbed a knife and kneed Singleton in the groin. It was during that struggle, a totally unpremeditated act, that Singleton eventually got possession of the knife and stabbed Hayes to death by accident.

That was a surprise. He was not even using a diminished capacity defense—that the defendant was too drunk to know what he was doing—and she was admitting her client's guilt, putting it right up front that while he was guilty of murder, it had not been premeditated.

Clearly, Menadier knew that the facts of the case and Singleton's background precluded raising reasonable doubt that the crime was committed by him. Better to admit right off the bat that he had done it. Lay it right out there for the jury to see, but make it clear that it wasn't premeditated. And if the jury bought that, they would have no choice but to come back with a not-guilty verdict on murder one, and guilty on murder two, thereby saving his life.

Of course, it was Singleton's version of the crime Menadier presented to the jury. Aware of that, the jury would then have to decide if Singleton was telling the truth.

With opening arguments concluded, the prosecution opened their case.

"Call Gene Reynolds to the stand," said Peden.

A mild-mannered man, Reynolds came forward through the slatted wooden gate, and was sworn in. He took his seat in the witness box, and when he was settled in, Michelle Peden asked him to describe what he had seen at Singleton's house on the afternoon of the murder.

Reynolds explained that he had gone over to Singleton's house, hoping to do some touch-up work on a previous paint job he had done at the ex-merchant marine's house. When he got to "Bill's" house—Singleton had told Reynolds that that was his name—he saw Hayes and Singleton seated on a couch. Both of them were "stark naked," Reynolds testified.

"I heard her gurgling 'Help,'" he continued, in a "weak, muffled" voice. Like watching an accident in slow motion, Reynolds was transfixed by the horror of it and yet powerless to do anything.

Alarmed, he ran from the house, grabbed a shovel, and was about to go back in the house when his uncle, who had accompanied him, stopped him. Instead, they went around to the other side of the house and peered through the window into the living room.

"He was standing over her with his hands on her neck," Reynolds continued.

Then Reynolds went around to the front door and kicked at it. Hearing the sound, Singleton, he said, looked in his direction. Twice. Hayes turned, too, and said something. He heard him tell Hayes, "Shut up, bitch!"

"Objection." And Menadier was on her feet.

"Your Honor, the witness never mentioned the word 'bitch' in his deposition."

In most states, all witnesses are deposed before they testify. Menadier then requested that the judge allow her to view Reynolds's grand jury testimony, which she previously had not been privy to.

Menadier's request put the judge in a bind. Because grand jury proceedings are supposed to be secret, he had to weigh revealing them versus the defendant's right to a fair trial. He decided to review Reynolds's grand jury testimony in camera (in private), and then rule on the defense attorney's request. In the meanwhile, Reynolds could continue testifying.

"What did you see next?" Michelle Peden asked him.

Reynolds said that as he continued to look in the house, he suddenly saw Singleton's arm rise up and plunge down, pounding on her head, neck, and chest.

"It sounded like bones crushing, like chicken bones breaking," he said.

Alarmed that something horrible was going on inside that they could not handle, Reynolds and his uncle drove to a nearby Chevron gas station and dialed 911. He reported what he had seen and expected the cops would arrive quickly. But after driving around for ten or fifteen minutes, they returned a second time to the house, only to find that the cops had not arrived yet. Only when they returned a third time did they find a sheriff's deputy, who had finally responded to the call.

There wasn't really much that Menadier could do on cross. Reynolds was positive of what he had seen. But he did admit that he never saw the deboning knife that the police said was the murder weapon.

In the jury's mind, Menadier left them with the thought that while

Reynolds had seen "pounding-like" motions, Singleton may have just been using his hands. For the jury to then find reasonable doubt, they would have to believe that while Reynolds went to call the cops, Singleton retired to another room, and someone else stole into the house and delivered the death blows.

After Reynolds finished his testimony, the prosecution called Deputy Paul Robbins to the witness stand. Robbins testified that he was the first officer to reach the house. He had just finished up an assignment in the Clair Mel section of the county when he heard the report of a "domestic disturbance" on his police radio and volunteered to take it because no other sector cars were available. He said that the delay in responding to the call was due to a shift change, heavy traffic, and a large number of 911 calls that evening.

When he arrived on the scene, it was 6:23 P.M., and he met Singleton at the carport doorway. Singleton had responded to his knock. Peden then wanted to know if there was anything unusual about the defendant.

"His genitals were hanging out," Robbins said, referring to the defendant's naked appearance.

"How did the defendant appear?"

"Nervous."

"Did he say anything?"

"He said that he was in a fuss or a spat with his girlfriend and everything was okay now," Deputy Robbins said. "He was insisting over and over again that everything was okay and I didn't need to be there."

Given the blood on Singleton and his state of undress, it was unlikely that Robbins would leave the scene.

"Did you ask him where the blood came from?"

"He said that he cut himself chopping turnips."

The officer said that just then, the telephone rang. Singleton ignored it, not seeming to hear the sound. When his neighbor Stu Simon pointed out that the phone was ringing, Singleton went inside to answer it. Robbins followed him and found Roxanne Hayes lying on the floor, her life's blood seeping out of her body.

TUESDAY, FEBRUARY 17

"Call Lee Miller to the stand," Peden said.

Miller came forward, took the oath from the court clerk, and took his seat in the witness box to the right of the judge. He was testifying as an expert witness.

In the first set of preliminary questions, that any expert is asked, Miller identified himself as the associate medical examiner of Hillsborough County. "I've conducted more than five thousand autopsies," he testified.

"Would you please describe the wounds to the decedent?" Peden requested, and Miller produced a graphic photo of the dead Hayes, her wounds evident.

Miller proceeded to describe and then point out seven stab wounds to the chest and abdomen. Specifically, a two-inch wound pierced Hayes's heart and caused her to bleed to death, though she probably remained conscious from five to twenty minutes before death. Two other wounds perforated her liver and one of those was " . . . six to seven inches deep," he testified. Miller then showed the jury photographs of Hayes's hands, on which it was obvious that she had deep cuts.

"How were those cuts caused?" Peden wondered.

"They were caused," Miller responded, "by Roxanne Hayes grabbing the knife blade in an [unsuccessful] effort to defend herself."

Such defense wounds were common in stabbing cases when the victim had an opportunity to fight back as Hayes did.

"These wounds," Miller added, "are consistent with her attacker standing over her, stabbing, as she struggled to survive."

Then Peden introduced a key piece of evidence: a photograph of Lawrence Singleton taken shortly after the crime was committed.

The years had not treated Singleton well. Like many of the retirees in Florida, he had a sagging belly, liver spots on hands and face, a balding head with fringes at the side. But he also had the nose of a drunk, reddish with burst veins, and the effect of that bulbous protuberance was to make him look like some punch-drunk fighter who had seen too much action. As for his body, Singleton was stark naked.

On his limp penis was a condom, the one he had used when he and Roxanne Hayes had sex, right before he killed her. His arms and legs had impressive muscles from the years of physical work as a merchant marine, but he was obviously growing soft from booze and age. His posture was slightly bent, arms that once had tied knots at sea in a seaman's expert manner, hung like dead weights. Still, he looked more than a match for the six foot, 170-pound Hayes.

Police had taken the picture for a reason. Singleton had made statements when he was arrested that he had been defending himself against Hayes. In case he claimed that at trial, they wanted the photo to prove that he had a nary a mark on him.

How could he struggle with Hayes, holding a knife no less, and not even have one cut on him, let alone a bruise?

Miller's testimony was gripping, graphic, and lethal. The photos showed what looked like a sexual deviant, and his victim, a woman killed in a horrible manner by a strong, seemingly cold-blooded killer. Menadier needed to temper the testimony in two ways.

First, she needed to use a tactic that lawyers used for rape trials: she needed to put the victim on trial, so that the jury would see her true character and lose their sympathy for her. Second, Menadier needed to show that the crime was absolutely, positively not premeditated, that essentially the victim and the accused were partying before the crime occurred.

"Dr. Miller, did the victim have cocaine in her system?" Menadier asked.

"Yes," Miller responded, "but there's no way to tell how long it had been there. She could have taken the drug from an hour to several days before her death."

"Dr. Miller, what did you find in the victim's stomach?"

Singleton had told Menadier that they had had dinner before the crime occurred. Miller said that Hayes had eaten beans, rice, and chicken thirty minutes to an hour before she died.

What kind of killer feeds his victim before killing her? Menadier hoped that in the jury's mind that would signal that the killing was actually an eruption of uncontrolled violence. In other words, second-degree murder.

After Miller finished his testimony, the state called Walter Brown, a sheriff's deputy who was on the scene the night of the murder.

"Did the defendant say anything to you about the events of that night?" the prosecutor asked.

Brown said that Singleton told him, "'We had an argument and she threw something at me so I killed her.'"

"Did he say anything else?"

"Yes, he said, 'I guess that makes me a murderer, so you've got me now.'"

It was damning testimony—the defendant admitting to the crime. The prosecution already had fifty percent of its work done because the defendant had admitted he did it. They didn't even have to prove it.

FOURTEEN

WEDNESDAY, FEBRUARY 18

The prosecution's case was drawing to a close, but they believed in the big-bang theory of conclusions.

"The prosecution calls Detective Larry Lingo."

A Hillsborough County sheriff's detective, Lingo was one of the first detectives on the scene the night of the murder. His role, however, was to testify as a narrator.

A television was wheeled over to the jury box and set right in front of the fourteen members of the panel. A videotape was popped into the machine, turned on, and suddenly, the crime scene burst to life in living color.

The camera moved through the beautiful new kitchen with its marbled counters, and into the bedroom where the bedclothes appeared in disarray. Suddenly, the camera moved into the living room. What the jury saw was the type of inflammatory material defense lawyers hate—a graphic tape of the crime scene.

"There's the victim," said Detective Lingo.

She was lying on Singleton's plush blue carpet stained red by her blood. Her eyes were open. The girlfriend, prostitute, and drug user, wearing no clothes, was posed in that awkward manner that could only mean death. Her legs were crossed at the ankles, and her hands hung limply at her side.

Blood was everywhere—on her face, chest, and stomach, spattered on the floor. She looked like a bloody animal that had been brought to the slaughter. Nearby was the knife that had allegedly inflicted the wounds and a length of rope. The camera then moved outside, where Singleton's van, the doors open, took up part of the driveway.

The jury watched intently, moving forward in their seats. The graphic images, accompanied by nothing but silence on the soundtrack, made for a spellbinding presentation. The expressions of anguish and sympathy on their faces were quite evident.

After the tape was finished, a second one was loaded up, the *start* button was pressed, and on came Singleton himself. It was after his arrest. He was wearing handcuffs, being led from the sheriff's homicide office shortly after he had been taken into custody. By that time, word had leaked out to the media of the sensational nature of the crime and the arrest. Local stations had sent camera crews, who shined their lights directly into his craggy, tired face. The *St. Petersburg Times* and *Tampa Tribune* dispatched their reporters to the scene, who peppered the former merchant seaman with question after question.

"Did you do it?"

"Did you kill Roxanne Hayes?"

"Why'd you do it, Larry?"

The questions kept coming. Looking directly into the camera, Singleton finally replied, "Yep, I done it."

"Why'd you do it, sir?" one reporter asked him.

Singleton shook his head. "I don't know" was his simple reply.

What the jurors did not see was the rest of the tape, where reporters continued asking questions, looking for Singleton's motivation.

"How come?"

"Why'd you do it?"

"They framed me the last time," Singleton replied, referring to his rape and mutilation of Mary Vincent. "This time, I did it."

The judge had made sure the comments were edited out, since the prosecutors were prohibited from disclosing Singleton's record to the jurors. The ones picked, in fact, had sworn that they knew nothing about Singleton's infamous California past. They would not have been seated had they admitted to that prior knowledge.

All through the presentation of the tapes, Singleton remained expressionless. It didn't seem to worry him that the prosecution was moving him closer and closer to the death chamber.

As their final witness, the prosecution put on Sheriff's Corporal Donald K. Bowling. Bowling had arrested Hayes numerous times. In fact, Hayes had an extensive arrest record stretching back ten years, ranging from prostitution to narcotics possession.

When asked what Hayes's demeanor was like, Bowling replied, "She was absolutely passive, nonviolent. Her business was being a professional prostitute. I've never known her to be a violent person."

The testimony was meant to head off any supposition on the part of the defense that Hayes was aggressive toward Singleton, which therefore would justify the homicide.

The prosecution then rested. Their side of the case was singular for its brevity, yet no less damning in its graphic details. After the recess, it would be the defense's turn.

The courtroom was rife with speculation over whether Singleton would testify or not. It was a double-edged sword. If he testified, he could try to present an alternative interpretation of the facts. But that also entailed opening himself up to what would certainly be a scathing cross-examination by the prosecution.

Regardless, public defenders Menadier and Skye had decided to pursue a strategy of showing the jury that Singleton was too depressed to form the requisite premeditation for first-degree murder.

"Call Stu Simon to the stand."

Singleton's neighbor, Stu Simon came forward, took the oath, and got into the witness box.

"Did you have any interaction with the defendant the week prior to Ms. Hayes's death?" Skye asked.

"Yes, I did," Simon answered.

Simon related how, in that previous week, he had saved Singleton from committing suicide by carbon monoxide poisoning. Singleton had attempted to run a hose from his exhaust into his car, where he sat waiting to inhale the fumes. Simon had pulled him out before he could do any lasting damage.

"Were you also on the scene the day of the murder?"

"Yes, I was."

Simon happened to show up right after the murder was committed.

"What kind of shape was the defendant in?" Skye wondered.

"He wasn't too steady on his feet. Bill looked like he was drunk."

The thought being implanted in the jurors minds was "Could a drunk man form the requisite intent for premeditated murder?"

THURSDAY, FEBRUARY 19

It was just over a year ago that Roxanne Hayes had died. Her ghost seemed to hover around the hushed, packed courtroom as her killer prepared to testify. Despite the risk, the defense had decided to let Singleton testify.

Lawrence Singleton had the face of a life-long drunk and rapist who had deteriorated to murder: bulbous, veined nose; a face etched with deep, craggy lines that on another man might have indicated character but on him, deterioration; and a mouth that looked like it could turn vile at a moment's notice.

Singleton was a rarity in today's criminal justice system: a murderer who wasn't young or middle-aged, but seventy years, old. He wasn't weak, though. He still had the strong hands and physique of a merchant seaman.

In the opinion of many, including the state of California and his first victim, Mary Vincent, he had never adequately paid for his crimes. The explanation for his crimes that he had offered then Sergeant Richard Breshears in 1978 was long behind him. Back then, he had just been trying to use his mouth to keep himself out of jail. Now, the stakes were higher, much higher, yet it was doubtful anyone in the courtroom, with the exception of his attorneys, felt any sympathy for him.

As for the reason he was testifying, his attorneys, Skye and Menadier, knew they didn't have much choice. They knew he wouldn't be the best of witnesses. They knew he looked like what he was. That couldn't be hidden, even under the sport jacket, slacks, shirt, and tie their client wore for the occasion.

They were losing. So at all costs, the jury needed to know Singleton's version of what had happened. Besides, they had nothing to lose. The prosecution had painted him as a vicious animal. The defense needed to show he was a human being, albeit flawed.

"Mr. Singleton, did you deliberately kill Roxanne Hayes?" Menadier asked.

"Ma'am, it was an accident," Singleton said, looking imploringly at the jury. "I swear on the Bible it was."

"How did you come to meet the decedent?"

"We met at a Kentucky Fried Chicken restaurant about two months ago. She joked around with me. I took her home and paid her twenty dollars for oral sex. I gave her my phone number."

"Did she call you?"

"Three weeks later. She wanted to know if I'd like her services again."

He would and she came over.

"How many more times did you meet afterwards?"

"Just that night."

"What happened the night Roxanne Hayes died?"

Quickly and efficiently, Singleton explained how ill he'd been feeling that day, how depressed he was. He had mixed fortified wine with a sleeping pill, an antidepressant, and an antihistamine. Clearly, he wasn't himself and feeling godawful.

Singleton went on to describe how he had picked Hayes up at her bus stop, as he had in the past. He hired her for sex and companionship. Then after they got to his house, things got out of hand.

He had always found Roxanne to be " . . . a lovely person. Nice to talk to. But I never seen her in a mood like that." Roxanne had gotten angry.

"She complained that the price of cocaine had gone up," Singleton said.

Because of that, she wanted more money for her services. When she grabbed Singleton's wallet to get it, and stuffed the cash in her mouth, "I got quite angry," he continued. They fought and she grabbed a large kitchen knife, one of two he had on the table for peeling potatoes in front of the TV.

"I was afraid for my own life, and I was trying to control the knife," Singleton said. "She threatened to cut my head off, and then took a swing at me. The knife was in her right hand."

Gesticulating wildly to show the jury how the fight had gone, Singleton described how they fought for possession of the weapon. Singleton managed to get a grip on the knife handle, which left only the blade for Hayes to grab.

"That's how she got those gashes on her hand," he said, though he failed to note why, if all he was trying to do was get the knife out of her hands, she gripped it so tightly that the blade cut right down to the bone.

"The knife went over my head and probably went right into her face," was how he described the wound to her face. As the struggle continued, he said, "Probably each time that I pushed her, the knife would go in," for a total of seven wounds. "I was just trying to get it down."

Singleton remembered that neither he nor Hayes said anything to the other during the struggle, which he estimated lasted just thirty seconds. The only sound was when he put his finger in her mouth to try to get the money she had secreted there.

"I screamed when she bit me. I had no idea and I had no way of knowing the damage was being done," he testified. Just like he couldn't figure out who had cut Mary Vincent's arms off. The question was: would the jury buy it?

"Did you have any intention of killing Roxanne, hurting her or anything like that?" Jill Menadier asked.

"No ma'am," Singleton answered fervently. "It was probably both of us doing it."

"What happened then?"

"I immediately thought of calling 911, but I didn't have the ability," Singleton said. "I picked up the television remote control, thinking it was the telephone. I told her we had to get to the hospital."

Gripping her around the shoulders, he helped her walk toward the door, but they only got as far as the dining room where she collapsed.

"I fell down beside her and I was crying."

He managed to get her onto the couch.

"And then?"

"Well, Roxanne, she sat on the blue-plaid couch in my living room, really bleeding. She put both arms around me and asked me to hold her. We were embracing. I held her tight. I sat there and cried and rubbed her face and tried to talk to her," he said. But it was no use because Hayes was dead.

In all of his testimony, that scene stood out as the strangest and probably the truest. It would be easy to imagine Hayes, her life slipping away, aware she was dying, reaching out to the only human being present, ironically the man who was about to become her murderer.

When Peden took over for cross, she wondered why the cut to Hayes's stomach was so deep, it went straight through to her spine. After all, if all Singleton was trying to do was disarm her, why stab her so viciously?

"That happened after she kneed me in the groin, ma'am," Singleton explained. "God's honest truth, I fell directly into her. She sat down on the couch and then I fell into her. That's that seven-inch wound."

"So you're saying that Roxanne Hayes stabbed herself?"

"It was probably both of us doing it," Singleton answered.

"You and her are combining rather forcefully to put the knife into her," Peden said in a mocking manner.

"Yes, that's what happened."

"You didn't see the cuts on her?" Peden asked incredulously. "She didn't start to bleed profusely?"

"Not that I recall," he said.

"Do you recall telling Deputy Robbins, the first deputy on the scene, that everything was okay, that you and your girlfriend had just had an argument?"

"I panicked," Singleton explained, as rationally as he could. "That was the last thing I wanted to do was have to explain to a policeman having a dead woman on my floor."

"Oh, Mr. Singleton, have you ever been convicted of a felony?"

Singleton paused and responded with a barely audible, "Yes."

"More than one?"

Pause. "Yes."

"No further questions."

Understandably, he declined to offer any details of those crimes. Had he done that, the jury would have heard about his mutilation of Mary Vincent.

There wasn't much more the defense could do. Who were they supposed to, put on as a character witness? Lobster Boy?

Joe Registrato, the chief public defender in Hillsborough County, had told this writer before the trial that had it been any other defendant, the state never would have asked for murder one and death. It was because of Singleton's record in California and, Registrato might have added, Florida was trying to rectify its decision to accept Singleton in the first place.

In his conversations with this writer, Registrato consistently talked about the penalty phase of the trial. It seemed a foregone conclusion that the jury would convict, and the real battleground would be pleading with the jury to keep Singleton out of the hot seat.

There had been a lot of controversy the previous year when a murderer was executed in Florida's electric chair and the black death mask that the condemned man wore caught fire. As witnesses continued to watch the man's face was seared to a crisp. The odor of burned flesh permeated the death chamber. The state, meanwhile, would not stop the execution just because the murderer was literally burning his way toward hell.

For Registrato, Menadier, Skye, and others who opposed the death penalty, that image of the death mask on fire, of the man's flesh melting, was a harbinger of the fate that awaited Singleton should their pleadings not be successful.

The job of prosecutors Peden and Pruner was directly at odd with the defense attorneys'. They wanted to get Singleton into that chair, and if his nose melted in the process, tough.

FIFTEEN

FRIDAY, FEBRUARY 20

As with all criminal cases in Florida, the prosecution began the closing arguments. Assistant State Attorney Jay Pruner delivered the close and he gave an impassioned one.

Pruner reviewed the known facts of the case and Singleton's culpability in Hayes's murder. He said that Singleton's claims that Hayes inflicted the death wounds on herself were preposterous.

"If you are to believe Lawrence Singleton, this lunatic, Roxanne Hayes became enraged and threatened to decapitate him." It was an utterly ridiculous argument. "If you're to believe Lawrence Singleton's testimony, the only crime he committed was assisting suicide." As for Singleton's account of tenderly holding the dying Hayes in his arms, Pruner said, "I'm sure it was a very touching moment for all of you, if you are able to believe Mr. Singleton," which he clearly believed they could not. Not unless they were lunatics.

"What the evidence shows you is that Mr. Singleton plunged that knife in seven times intentionally," Pruner continued.

Clearly, Singleton was a wanton criminal, a murderer who snuffed out Roxanne Hayes's life in a calculated act, Pruner told them. In reminding the jury of the bloody murder scene, including the angle of the stab wounds on her hands that were consistent with her attacker standing over her and thrusting the knife downward, Pruner characterized the murder as the most heinous brutality imaginable.

"Your only choice, your only choice is to come back with a verdict of murder in the first degree." Pruner sat down and gave the stage to the defense.

"We have never attempted for even one moment to say that Larry Singleton was not responsible for what happened to Roxanne Hayes and I'm not going to insult your intelligence by doing that now," defense attorney Jill Menadier told the jury. "Lawrence Singleton never, never at any time made a decision to kill Roxanne Hayes. Larry Singleton did not have an ounce of ill will, hatred, or spite toward Roxanne Hayes."

Instead, her death was the result of a deadly combination of antidepressants, alcohol, and an antihistamine Singleton took the day of the murder. He was not in his right mind or in control of his actions. The murder Lawrence Singleton committed was "a spontaneous eruption of emotion." Therefore, the jury had no choice but to find that it was not a calculated, premeditated act, and had to come in with a verdict of not guilty on murder one. Murder two, yes, even murder three if they were so generous, but murder one—no way. The prosecution hadn't proved their case.

After Menadier sat down, the judge charged the jury. He explained the necessary legal components to convict on murder one, and gave the jury the option to convict on the lesser charges. By then, it was midday, and he excused the jury to have lunch and begin their deliberations.

A jury could be out a few hours, a few days, or longer. To everyone involved in the case, it was a time of great tension.

While Singleton cooled his heels in a holding cell below the courtroom, the lawyers roamed the corridors, sometimes going back to their offices, which were on the upper floors of the courthouse.

In the media room, reporters hung around, reading papers and paperbacks. The TV correspondents put on their makeup for live updates downlinking via the satellite antennas attached to their trucks parked outside the courthouse. The print reporters waited, too, hoping the verdict would come in time to meet their evening deadlines for the next day's paper.

Just two hours and forty minutes later, the phone rang in the state's attorney's office.

"There's a verdict," said the court clerk.

He hung up the phone and dialed the public defender's line.

"There's a verdict," he repeated.

All the lawyers hustled back into the courtroom. Singleton was brought in from the holding cell, the reporters sat with pencils poised over paper. In the back of the courtroom, photographers and a video crew shooting for all the local stations focused their cameras, getting ready for the singular shot of the defendant reacting to the verdict.

"Mr. Foreman, I understand you've reached a verdict?"

"Yes, we have Your Honor," said the foreman.

The verdict was written on a single sheet of folded, white paper that the foreman handed to the court clerk. The court clerk read the verdict.

"On the sole count, murder in the first degree, we find the defendant guilty!"

As the verdict was read, the only emotion Lawrence Singleton showed was to rapidly blink his eyes. Then he nodded at the judge.

"The sentencing phase of this trial will begin Monday," said Judge Mitcham, who motioned the bailiffs to take Singleton into custody. Chains were attached to his wrists and ankles and he was led off, taking baby steps into the bowels of the building.

Roxanne Hayes's boyfriend, Fred Ricker, was in the courtroom with their children: Xena, the oldest at twelve, who had decided that she would become a lawyer and prosecute men like Singleton; Ricker, eight, the middle child; and the baby, four-year-old Malachi. All were dressed in black to denote their continued mourning. As the verdict was read, Ricker hugged them close and he began to cry.

Sitting there throughout the trial, they had all heard the evidence about their mother participating in the world's oldest profession. That hadn't bothered them so much as the people judging them on the basis of her actions.

Xena had saved a letter to the editor of one of the local papers critical of Roxanne, in which she and her siblings were described disparagingly as "illegitimate."

"I'm saving it 'til I graduate and when I make valedictorian," said Xena.

Outside, Ricker addressed reporters at an impromptu press conference. He said he was thankful that the jurors had rejected the defense's efforts to characterize Hayes as something less than a human being.

"The jury looked through the smoke and saw the facts. Roxie wasn't a thief. She never hurt anybody. Roxanne had a name," he told the reporters afterward. "They looked at Roxanne as being somebody. We've been hearing prostitute, thief. She was a *human being*."

Regardless of the way she was portrayed by Singleton, Roxanne Hayes was a good mother. She would take her kids on trips to the park, swimming at the Y, dress them up on Halloween, everything a good mother would do. She even broke her cocaine habit when she was pregnant.

Ricker had taken to higher ground. He and the kids were now part of a regular church congregation. His goal was at some point in the future to become a preacher. God had become an important part in their lives. Still, He couldn't take away the pain.

"Think Singleton should go to the chair?" a reporter shouted at Ricker.

Ricker didn't believe anyone should die in the electric chair. Still, he made sure to add that he didn't want Singleton "to ever harm another soul again."

"How'd your girlfriend's murder affect your children?" a second reporter asked.

"He killed a big part of them," Ricker answered simply, nodding at his three children. "But we forgive him."

MONDAY, FEBRUARY 23

Jason McCord, a gun salesman, had been convicted of sexual assault in 1990, and sentenced to life in prison. But his case was overturned on appeal, and he worked out an arrangement where he pleaded to a reduced charge, got only one more year in jail and then probation.

He had been at the courthouse for a few days, working on a motion in his case. Representing himself, McCord planned to file another appeal. Out in the corridor between legal proceedings, McCord, like everyone else, became aware of who the Singleton jurors were while they took breaks in the trial. They stayed to themselves, a tight-knit bunch, well aware of their responsibility in a capital murder case.

During a break before the judge's charge, McCord had approached Tom Brewster, one of the twelve Singleton jurors. He was standing, sipping a cup of coffee when McCord sidled up to him.

"Hey," said McCord.

Brewster just smiled, wishing this guy would vanish.

"So how you going to vote? I mean after you convict him?"

"Huh?"

"You gonna vote for death or not?"

Stunned that anyone would be so brazen, and so stupid, to ask him what he had sworn to keep secret, Brewster still didn't reply; then McCord added, "Just make sure you do the right thing."

Since the judge wasn't available over the weekend, Monday morning bright and early, Brewster had reported the conversation to the bailiff, who relayed it to the judge.

Mitcham immediately called Brewster into his chambers and questioned him about the identity of the man who approached him, as well as whether or not the conversation had prejudiced Brewster's ability to render a sentencing recommendation that was not biased by the conversation.

"Your Honor, the guy who approached me is an idiot. I can certainly continue nonprejudiced."

Mitcham could see that Brewster was telling the truth and made the decision to continue proceedings. Otherwise, if Brewster had been thrown off the jury, it would have been a mistrial, because the alternates had been dismissed after the verdict.

Judge Mitcham called McCord into his chambers.

"Don't you ever do that again," he told McCord, obviously relieved that this trial, unlike the first, was running toward its conclusion.

TUESDAY, FEBRUARY 24

There was a delay in the penalty phase of the trial. The prosecution had to fly their star witness in from Tacoma, Washington, where she lived with her boyfriend.

Not since July 18, 1994, had there been as much anticipation in the Hillsborough County courthouse on Twiggs Street. On that date, defense attorney Arnold Levine called to the stand "Little" Grady Stiles, in the Lobster Boy murder case. Singleton's old drinking buddy had been murdered. Little Grady's stepmother, Mary Teresa Stiles, was on trial for ordering a hit on her husband, Lobster Boy himself, Grady Stiles, Jr.

Little Grady and Grady, Jr., shared a birth defect that gave them what looked like lobster claws for hands and feet. The senior Stiles had made a small fortune off his birth defect as a sideshow freak. But what the public never realized was that Stiles, whose upper body was overdeveloped from having to use his hands as feet, was stronger than any two men. And he had used his cruel strength, Levine claimed, to abuse his wife to the point that she was so battered, she couldn't stand it any more and hired a hit man to kill Stiles.

After Little Grady took the stand by sliding from his wheelchair into the box, Levine deliberately made him get out of the box and put on a hand-walking demonstration for the jury. In this way, Levine hoped to establish Little Grady's strength and by extension, his father's.

The hand-walking stunt had been the highlight of a bizarre trial that not only included testimony from the members of the Lobster family but also "Midget Man," a dwarf who had also been married to Mary Stiles.

Now, the courthouse braced for the testimony of another "freak," only this time, the deformity was man made.

The prosecution had sent Mary Vincent a ticket and provided her with a hotel room so she could come to Florida and testify against Singleton. It was an opportunity to get revenge, to see that the man who had mutilated her once and for all was taken off the planet.

"Separated by twenty years and thousands of miles, two women unrelated except by their tragic connection to Lawrence Singleton, got into Mr. Singleton's van," prosecutor Jay Pruner said in his opening statement of the penalty phase of the trial.

"Mary Vincent accepted a ride in 1978. Some twenty years later, Roxanne Hayes got into a van driven by Mr. Singleton and she, unlike Mary Vincent, did not survive her meeting."

Based upon Singleton's record of barbarity, he argued that Singleton should be sentenced to death.

When it was his turn, John Skye pointed at Singleton. The killer was wearing a rumpled jail uniform.

"He is an old man, now in the only clothes he will ever wear again. This trial is not a matter of vengeance, or for you to clean up California's mistakes from twenty years ago, but about whether that old man dies a natural death or we take him out and kill him. And that would not be justice. It would demean us all."

In effect, what Skye was saying was that Singleton was such a loser, he was just not worth executing.

After opening statements, Pruner called his first witness.

"The state calls Mary Vincent."

In the media room, reporters adjusted their monitors, making sure their video would be pristine for the evening news. In the courtroom, the video camera whirred and still-camera shutters clicked as Vincent was ushered into the courtroom by the bailiff.

Vincent had changed much from twenty years before. Once, she had looked like an innocent fifteen-year-old, but the thirty-five-year-old woman who came into the courtroom looked far from innocent.

She was slightly hunched over, either from the weight of years, the weight of her prostheses, or both. She had an open, though pained, face, with lines of grief etched into her skin. With haunted brown eyes, she barely looked at Singleton.

She had on a worn cardigan sweater over an old T-shirt, stained sweat pants, no socks, and weathered, dirty sneakers. She sat down in the witness box and Pruner began his direct examination.

"Could you tell us how you came to make the defendant's acquaintance?" Pruner began.

All eyes in the courtroom were transfixed by her metal claws. Actually, they were much more than that.

The arm itself was made of Fiberglas, like the kind used to make boats. Two curves of metal made up her aluminum hook. One part moved, while the other remained immobile. The movable part was attached to a wire cable that ran up her arm, connected to a fabric harness that was worn over the opposite shoulder. When the shoulder was flexed, the cable was pulled, and the hook could open or close.

They were the same type of arms that Harold Russell had worn as a handicapped serviceman in the classic film *The Best Years of Our Lives*. It wasn't so much that prosthetic developments had stagnated since then; there were artificial limbs available that used electronic impulses to make the arms work, prostheses reminiscent of the ones worn by Lindsay Wagner as *The Bionic Woman*. But the cost had made such devices out of Mary's reach. Plus there was an even more important factor.

Mary had always been afraid Singleton might get out and attack her again. If that ever happened, her claws could be a deadly defensive weapon.

Vincent proceeded to offer a terse, though detailed, account of how she had met Singleton, but was interrupted when Judge Mitcham realized she had not taken the oath. He stopped her from speaking.

"Please raise your right arm and swear to tell the truth," Mitcham requested.

Mary was so broke, having been forced to declare bankruptcy in 1995, that when her right arm needed servicing, she couldn't afford the repairs and had to use a piece of yarn to fix the prothesis. That just made the arm weaker. She had use her lift hook to lift her arm. Only then could she swear the oath. The jury, of course, was watching all of this happening.

"Now, as you were saying," Pruner continued, "after you met Lawrence Singleton."

She described the trip they took in his van, and the drinking that took place on the way to Modesto. After that, "I was raped and I had my hands cut off," Vincent said in a quiet, deliberate voice. "He used a hatchet and left me to die."

But she had refused to die and, instead, had crawled almost two miles before she found help.

"Do you see the man who raped and cut off your forearms in this court today?" Pruner asked dramatically.

"I do," Vincent answered, and quickly, she raised her shiny metal claw and pointed it at Singleton, who sat emotionlessly at the defense table.

"That's the man who hurt me. Lawrence Singleton."

"No further questions."

John Skye was on his feet quickly. He couldn't allow the jury to think about what they had just heard. He needed to get away from the emotional effect she was obviously having on the jury.

"Was Mr. Singleton drinking before the attack?"

"Yes."

"What was he drinking?"

"Vodka from a plastic gallon jug during the attack."

"Did he continue drinking" throughout his attack on her? Skye wanted to know.

"It's hard to recall," she answered.

After all, not only was she in tremendous shock from loss of blood and the savagery of the assault, it had taken place twenty years before.

Skye's goal was to establish Singleton's lifelong pattern of drinking and then violence, cause and effect. Other than doing that, there really wasn't much else he could get out of the witness. Besides, if he was seen by the jury to be pressing her, it would only work against Singleton. Regardless of what they thought of Singleton and his actions, how could they not have sympathy for the poor woman?

After her testimony, the judge took a break, and the media followed Mary into the corridor outside Judge Mitcham's courtroom.

"How did you feel identifying the man who cut your arms off?" one reporter asked, rather crassly.

Vincent didn't blink. "I had to. I had to identify him," she responded. "I think I felt I had to testify."

"How are you today?" a second reporter asked politely, scratching out his notes.

"I'm still trying to stay alive," Vincent answered. "For the most part, I'm just trying to be a normal person."

Which certainly was a laudatory goal, but considering her mutilation, difficult to accomplish.

"How are you affected emotionally by this whole proceeding?" a third reporter asked.

"I blocked it out," she answered honestly. "I can't handle stress right now."

"What about the sentencing? You think he should get the chair?" the first reporter asked.

"Well, I'd rather not comment right now. I wouldn't want to say or do anything that might hurt the state's case."

Left unsaid was her fervent hope that this would be the end of Larry Singleton, the man who had ruined her life. She had still been trying to reap some benefit from that ruin, by selling her life story to a New York publisher. Despite the efforts of her and her boyfriend, no one was buying.

Like many who are the victim, Vincent believed that people all over the country would be interested in buying her story. She forgot to realize that she was competing with people like Monica Lewinsky and O. J. Simpson, who really commanded the national stage. While her case had been big in California, and she was trotted out every few years by overly aggressive politicians who wanted mandatory sentencing laws tightened, Mary Vincent was old news. Maybe with Singleton's sentence, she could finally find peace and put her past behind her.

SIXTEEN

Defense testimony was rather brief. Two of Singleton's neighbors testified that they liked him, even after discovering his awful past. A psychologist testified that Singleton suffered from dementia, that he was a lifelong alcohol abuser, and that he had an extreme anger toward women.

That was it. There really wasn't much in the way of extenuating circumstances. Skye had to count on the jury's mercy, that they would not want to put an old man into the death chamber. Jay Pruner, though, in his closing argument, saw things in a much more practical way. He asked the jurors to forget about Singleton's age and recommend a sentence of death.

"Lawrence Singleton is an old, mean-spirited drunk, who hates women, and has pickled his brain through alcoholism," Pruner concluded. "Common sense would tell you that."

Pruner said that he brought Vincent in from across space and time, dragged her out of the past, because he wanted them to see that Singleton had mutilated and raped a real human being two decades before.

"The fact of the matter is that twenty years ago, Lawrence Singleton did not dismember a document and leave a document for dead along a California roadside. He did not do that to a document, but to a human being."

Pruner pointed to pictures of Vincent's missing limbs and the deep defensive wounds on Roxanne Hayes's hands.

"You need look no further than the hands of those two women upon which Mr. Singleton wreaked havoc," to reach the verdict, he finished eloquently.

When it became the defense's turn to plead for Singleton's life, John Skye did the best he could in trying to sway the jury's mindset.

Skye described his client as a "ruined old man. He will be held responsible when he's put in a cage for the rest of his life." Better for him to die lonely in prison, he argued, than in the death chamber.

At the defense table, Singleton wiped tears from his eyes.

"Rather than hearing a news story about how the state of Florida fried Lawrence Singleton, we can hear a story like this: Lawrence Singleton died in his jail cell today, lonely and alone and despised," Skye concluded.

Once again, the judge charged the jury and made it clear that this sentencing hearing was different from the trial that had preceded it. All that was necessary to condemn Singleton to the electric chair was a majority vote. But if they so chose, they could also recommend a sentence of life in prison.

As the jury retired to consider their life-or-death decision, the courtroom buzzed with anticipation. Would the jury come back as quickly as before, despite the even more serious nature of their present deliberations? Or, would they take their time as they weighed Singleton's fate?

The time was five o'clock. There wasn't even time to run out and get a hamburger. Or a Coke. Maybe a cigarette, but that was about it.

One hour later, at six o'clock, the jury came back in. Lawyers, reporters, bailiffs, the court clerk, the judge, court watchers, all ran to take their places. Singleton, in shackles, sat down at the defense table. He licked his lips in anticipation.

"Ladies and gentleman, I understand you have concluded your deliberations?"

"Yes we have, Your Honor," said the foreman, handing the sentencing recommendation to the court clerk, who then handed it to the judge. He glanced at it, then asked Singleton to stand.

"Mr. Singleton," the judge began, "by a vote of ten to two, the jury recommends death."

Singleton didn't show any emotion. He was probably expecting the decision, perhaps even welcoming the executioner's jolt. He'd finally be free of the demons that had been dogging him all his life.

Shackles hobbling him, Lawrence Singleton shuffled away, following the guards, and exiting through a side entrance to the courtroom.

The lawyers approached the bench.

"We'll set sentencing for March thirtieth," said Judge Mitcham. Neither side objected.

After the hearing, an impromptu press conference was set up one more time outside the courtroom. While Skye and Menadier expressed disappointment with the jury's decision, Pruner and Peden claimed victory.

Six of the jurors agreed to meet the press.

"We knew we were about to make a decision no one wants to make," said juror Gertrude Klein.

"It was so one-sided," added juror Keith Racow.

"He was a monster," foreman Sal Hodges told the press. "There's no other way to describe him. After seeing Ms. Vincent, there's no other way to describe him."

"I think I'll be having nightmares for a long time," juror Tom Brewster added. "I was totally in shock when she walked into the courtroom and pointed one of her . . . uh . . . arms at Singleton."

As for that picture of Singleton standing alone, naked, wearing a condom, "shocking" was the only word to describe their joint reaction.

"I think he has shown and has proven himself to be a very evil human being, who has, in effect, taken away two lives," said a fifth juror, Archie Graham. "And what I want to know is how do you accidentally stab someone seven times?"

"The preponderant evidence was the stabbing seven times," answered the sixth juror, James Matson.

"Those knives were placed there on purpose," Brewster continued. "His wallet never left his pocket—so much for that crap about her trying to rob him. He knew exactly what he was doing. This man hated women."

"Mary Vincent's testimony was really moving," said Hodges.

"He destroyed her," Brewster concluded. "You can almost say that he killed two women."

"But we tried him on the Florida case, not the California case," Hodges was quick to add.

"I'm having flashbacks from looking at the picture of Roxanne dead," said Brewster. "There's no getting away from those pictures."

The others looked at him sympathetically.

"Know what bothers me the most?" Graham asked quietly.

The others looked at him.

"That rope. It was a small detail in one of the photos, remember? She was lying on the floor dead and this small piece of rope was on the floor beside her. What was that rope for?"

"That rope was to dispose of the body, like the prosecutor said," Brewster answered. And that conjured up the grisly murder, with all the details, finally complete.

There was Singleton, angry at Hayes, but really angry at all the women in his life. With each thrust of the knife, he obliterated one bad image after another. He was purifying his soul in the blood of a hapless hooker with a heart of gold. Really.

After Hayes was dead, he had tried attaching the rope to her ankle. He'd put her in the van outside and dispose of the body. But he was too drunk and too weak to make much of a go at it.

He gazed down at the dead woman on the carpet, and then he heard the doorbell. Not even cognizant that he was naked, with his flaccid penis still encased in a condom, and covered with the woman's blood, he went to answer the door.

"Yeah?"

It was a cop. Just what he needed right now, a cop asking questions why he had a dead girl on the floor in the other room.

He tried to send the cop away, but the officer followed him into the house and the next thing Singleton knew, he was up against the wall, and the guy was cuffing him. This time Singleton knew he wouldn't beat the rap.

Outside, a TV crew shined a light in his eyes!

"They framed me the last time," Singleton told them, referring to Mary Vincent. "This time, I did it."

What the hell was he talking about? thought a reporter. He looks like just a mean old drunk who killed a whore. A nobody from no place.

There was nothing very important about him. He would just get a few seconds on the evening news. It would never be anything bigger.

MARCH 30, 1998

Dressed once more in an orange prison jump suit, shackled at the hands and feet, Lawrence Singleton was taken across the street from the county jail to a holding cell inside the bowels of the Hillsborough County courthouse on Twiggs Street.

Soon, the bailiffs escorted him into the courtroom, where his lawyers, Skye and Menadier met him. Across the defense table sat prosecutor Jay Pruner. Then Judge Mitcham came in to begin the sentencing proceeding. It was Lawrence Singleton's last chance to escape the death chamber.

The prosecution argued for death one final time. As for Skye, he tried to pull a rabbit out of his legal bag.

"What everybody wants to happen here," said Skye in a ringing voice, "is to kill Mr. Singleton for what he did twenty years ago. That's not right. That's not fair. That's not the law. That's revenge."

After Skye had finished, the judge asked Fred Ricker if he had anything to say. Ricker said that he had forgiven Singleton and did not want to see him executed.

"When he killed Roxanne, he killed a part of me and my kids. He killed a great part of us. But we forgive him."

Later he would tell the press, "Any time a person is killed, or dies, it's not a happy thing. There's nothing for me to be happy about. There's nothing for anyone to be happy about."

That left only one person to be heard from. All along Singleton had said he had killed Hayes in self-defense. When given the opportunity, would he recant and throw himself on the mercy of the court to save his life?

"Mr. Singleton," Judge Mitcham urged, "do you have anything to say?"

Singleton stood up.

"Yes, Your Honor, I do."

"Go ahead."

"I'm sorry about the death in this case," he said in a halting voice. "I'll have to carry it on my conscience the rest of my life."

Not exactly a ringing confession rife with contrition. But at least it was something. Mitcham decided to delay sentencing until April 14. Singleton was taken back across the street to Hillsborough County Jail to await his judgment day.

For Mary Vincent, Singleton's conviction and sentencing was the end of a long van ride into hell. For twenty years, she could not look at her new "hands" without feeling fear that Singleton would be coming back. But now, she could wake up in the morning, look at her arms, and know that Lawrence Singleton was getting what he deserved.

After Singleton's arrest in 1997 for killing Hayes, the *Today* show had flown her to New York to appear live on national TV and to describe the attack and her continuing ordeal. *Today* did not pay her for her appearance, as was the custom with any journalistic endeavor. After that, Mary clammed up for the media. She made it known through her bodyguard and confidante, that her story was available, but only for the right price. She wouldn't give it away for free anymore. But 1978 was a long time ago; there were no takers. Ironically, the Mad Chopper was more famous than his victim, whose name was known by few. Fate then conspired to deal her a better break.

The publicity surrounding Singleton's arrest and conviction had been enormous. Reporters asked Lawrence Preston, an attorney who had worked with Mary during her civil suit against Singleton, where contributions could be sent. He gave them an address, and suddenly, by the hundreds, people, who felt Mary Vincent's pain, began sending her money. Typical was the contribution of John Russell.

Russell had read about Vincent in an edition of his local paper in Provo, Utah. Though he was an eighty-eight-year-old retiree on a fixed income, Russell was moved by Vincent's plight. He sent her a note on a piece of lined, loose-leaf paper, saying he and his ninety-three-year-old wife, Martha, wanted to help. They enclosed four twenty-dollar bills, indicating it was part of their Social Security benefits.

"I immediately went to the Pacific Northwest and offered to help set up a trust fund, free of charge," Preston told the Associated Press. "I could see that she was visibly moved by the amount of correspondence and the very personal tone of it."

Preston gave Mary some of the money from the fund for basic expenses, including rent and utilities. Preston had also managed to contact companies that specialized in making prosthetic limbs, and one of them, NovaCare of Oklahoma City, offered help. They sent a team to Seattle to talk with Mary about the new technology available in artificial limbs that they could provide on a less-than-cost basis. And while they were at it, they repaired her old arms.

"Obviously, we'll have to pay them something, but they're willing to work with her because of her plight," Preston continued.

There was the possibility the money could be used to provide a better life for her children. That's all Mary really wanted, to take care of her two kids. Maybe now, without having to worry about Singleton, she could spend more of her time with them. With a little money left over, maybe she could buy those new hands.

Regardless of what the future held in store for her, one thing Mary Vincent now knew for certain: Lawrence Singleton would never hurt another woman, *ever*. She could finally sleep well again at night.

Be it life in prison, or death, either way Lawrence Singleton would not be sailing the high seas again. Not in this life anyway.

SEVENTEEN

After the rape and assault on Mary Vincent, the California courts had given Lawrence Singleton a second chance. He was only sixty years old when he was released from prison, and he had a chance to live out his remaining years in relative harmony when he returned to Florida. And he did, for almost ten years.

Singleton had spent a lot of his time at the local bowling alley, tending his garden, and doing general improvements on his property. But those old sexual urges just wouldn't leave him alone.

Lawrence Singleton clearly, felt most comfortable with prostitutes, whom he didn't have to relate to on an emotional level. He had viewed Roxanne Hayes that way, and then that day in February, 1997, she became a human being to him, a human being on whom he could take out all his past anger toward women. When that paroxysm of rage was over, she lay dead on his living room floor.

Now, Singleton found himself back once more in the courtroom, where he had been convicted of the prostitute/mother's death. Had Roxanne been just any prostitute, the case wouldn't warrant the national attention it was receiving. But because she was the victim of Lawrence Singleton, the pervert who had chopped off the hands of that nice little girl in California almost twenty years ago, all along the newswire, Associated Press editors were waiting for word on what would happen in that Florida courtroom.

Would the court spare Singleton again, or would this time be Singleton's last?

APRIL 14, 1998

"All rise," the court clerk ordered.

As one, the people in the courtroom rose as Judge Mitcham took his seat high up on the bench then sat back down. All the players were assembled one last time. In addition to the prosecution and defense lawyers and the defendant, the courtroom was packed with reporters, and what few seats that were left went to lucky rubberneckers, the same type of people who slow down to watch at accident scenes.

"Mr. Singleton, would you stand please?" Judge Mitcham ordered.

In his bright orange jump suit, Singleton rose at the defense table and stared up at the judge.

"This was an unprovoked, senseless killing of a human being, the mother of lovely children, without cause, provocation, or justification," Mitcham began. Then he added a Biblical reference. "This killing further exemplifies that we are living in times worse than Sodom and Gomorrah."

Mitcham had referred to the Biblical cities that were so sinful, they were destroyed by God in a great conflagration, even as the just man Lot fled with his wife, who was turned to salt when she turned to watch the destruction. But unlike Lot, Mitcham was empowered. He was not about to turn into a bag of salt any time soon.

"Roxanne Hayes fought for her life. She literally clawed for her life. She was acutely aware of her impending death. The fact that the victim was a prostitute in no way diminished her right to life or justifies the taking of her life.

"Mr. Singleton"—and now Mitcham looked down from the bench like an avenging God from heaven—"you deserve no more chances.

I sentence you to death for the murder of Roxanne Hayes. And may God have mercy on your soul." Or at least more than you had on Mary Vincent, he might have added.

Singleton took a sharp breath, but showed no other reaction to the death warrant. He just stared out into space. Perhaps he was contemplating his own mortality. And just like that, without fanfare, the sentencing was over. Once again, a shackled, defeated ex-merchant marine, murderer/mutilator/rapist was hustled out into the bowels of the building, and now, the Florida State prison system.

As he left court, Fred Ricker reiterated, "I'm against the death penalty. It's sad that Mr. Singleton has to face the death penalty. We forgive him," His children stood beside him on the courthouse steps. "He has a greater punishment beyond the grave. But as long as he was in prison for life, that would have been enough for me."

Musing further, Ricker felt that the judge's sentence signified that "It is a recognition that her life was important. She was a human being. Roxanne has been recognized as a *person*."

Vincent was immediately contacted after the sentencing. A press conference was organized.

"I didn't want to play God and don't want anyone's death on my hands," she told reporters nervously. But she had no need for nerves; they were taking down and recording her every word. Even if she recited "Mother Goose," it would make the evening news.

"I am relieved that there has been justice served. I think I can start all over and put everything behind me and hopefully be safe and happy. I think there's a little bit of relief," Vincent continued. "I think we can *all* put this behind us now. I feel peace."

Vincent reminded reporters that people said she was paranoid when she told them that Singleton had told her that he was "'... going to finish the job.' I don't think I was paranoid enough."

She spoke of getting on with her life, of getting a job where she could "help people . . . so they don't have to go through what I went through."

Someone asked her how she had gotten through the dark years of learning to live with her disability.

"My children," she answered quickly. "Life. I love life, I really love life."

She could even joke about her condition. It seemed that on the way back home from Florida, the airline had lost some of her bags—the ones containing her second set of artificial arms.

"Half of me," she said, "is somewhere else."

After the death sentence, Singleton was taken outside, and placed in a van. He was driven upstate to Florida State Prison, where he took up residence on death row.

Of the thirty-eight states that have capital punishment, only five, besides Florida, require the electric chair—Alabama, Georgia, Kentucky, Nebraska, and Tennessee. Of the rest, most use the more humane method of lethal injection.

Singleton's sentencing coincided with the one-year anniversary of Florida's electric chair setting a convicted killer's death mask on fire. Eventually, an investigation placed the blame for the malfunction on the executioner's failure to properly apply electricity-conducting sponges in the chair's headpiece.

With blame adequately fixed, the state didn't have to go to the expense of buying a new three-legged, oak death contraption. Even a law suit challenging the use of the electric chair on constitutional grounds fell short of changing things, when the state supreme court upheld the use of the electric chair by a four-to-three vote in the fall of 1997. Still, the national attention was unwelcome in a state that preferred to be known for the round-trip rides through Disney-world rather than the one-way trip to the executioner. The state legislature decided to consider the matter of switching execution methods to lethal injection.

Not surprisingly, considering its conservative nature, the legislature on March 18, 1998, voted unanimously to keep electrocution as the state's method of execution.

Appeal in a capital case is mandatory in Florida, as it is in every state where capital punishment exists. Assuming there were no procedural irregularities, chances were Singleton's case would not be overturned on appeal. Few cases in Florida are. He also could not count on the governor granting clemency. What politician of either party, in his right mind, would grant clemency to "the Mad Chopper," regardless of Singleton's age?

Various state and federal laws over the past couple of years had been passed to decrease the time it took for the appeals process. Still, the average amount of time an inmate spent on Florida's death row was ten and a half years before he was executed. The oldest inmates at the time of Singleton's sentencing were Raymond Thomason, sixty-eight, and William Cruse, Jr., seventy.

Even if his appeal took only a few years, that was time enough for Singleton to continue drinking himself into liver failure on the homemade, two-hundred-proof alcoholic brews popular in prisons.

Maybe his abused liver would save the state the cost of an execution. Or maybe he'd play the string out with last-minute appeals until finally, with all of them exhausted, Lawrence Singleton would be marched into the death chamber. The electricity-conducting sponges would be applied to his ankles and resembling an ancient football helmet, the headpiece would then be strapped tightly over his head and secured beneath his chin with a worn leather strap. His hands and arms would be strapped down by the same, tough straps, and a black mask placed over his face. A heart monitor lead would be attached to his chest, and the lead stretched through the wall to a physician, who would monitor his heart action until the state was certain it had stopped.

The warden would read Singleton the death warrant, ask for any last words, and then, all would leave the old man alone. After a fleeting moment, the executioner would throw the switch and 10,000 volts of electricity would course through Singleton's body for approximately sixty seconds. Then the switch would be thrown "off," only to be flicked again into the "on" position, to make sure the job was done. After 10,000 volts lit him up, the machine would be turned off. The doctor would check his heart and if it was stopped, the body would be removed to a local mortuary where the family could claim it. If on the happenstance that Singleton was alive—and he is a tough old bird—they'd give him as many doses of "juice" as needed until he was dead.

EPILOGUE

There's an old saying: you can't keep a good man down. The same might be said for the opposite of the breed.

Three days after Singleton's death sentence, he was back in the news. It seemed that Larry, ever the avuncular sort, had made a good friend in prison: Willy Sexton, the son of Eddie Lee Sexton.

The elder Sexton, the subject of Lowell Cauffiel's recent book *House of Secrets*, was an Ohio man accused of incest and charged with ordering a family killing. Sexton listed Singleton as a witness for his July 13 trial.

Eddie Lee Sexton had previously been convicted in 1994 of ordering his son, Willie, to strangle another family member. An appeals court later overturned Eddie Lee's conviction and death sentence, maintaining that the jury should not have heard specific testimony regarding the bizarre life of the Sexton family.

Willie Sexton had only recently made a deal with prosecutors. He would plead guilty to second-degree murder and testify against his father.

Singleton and Willie had gotten tight while spending time together in the Hillsborough County Jail. "We believe that [Singleton] has information that will support our position that Eddie Sexton is not guilty of first-degree murder," said Sexton's attorney, Rick Terrana.

Singleton "developed a close relationship with Willie in jail," Terrana continued. Terrana had talked extensively with Singleton but would not disclose what he had to say.

So with it all, Lawrence Singleton may have found a get-out-of-jail card—albeit a limited one—and another shot at the spotlight.

IMAGE GALLERY

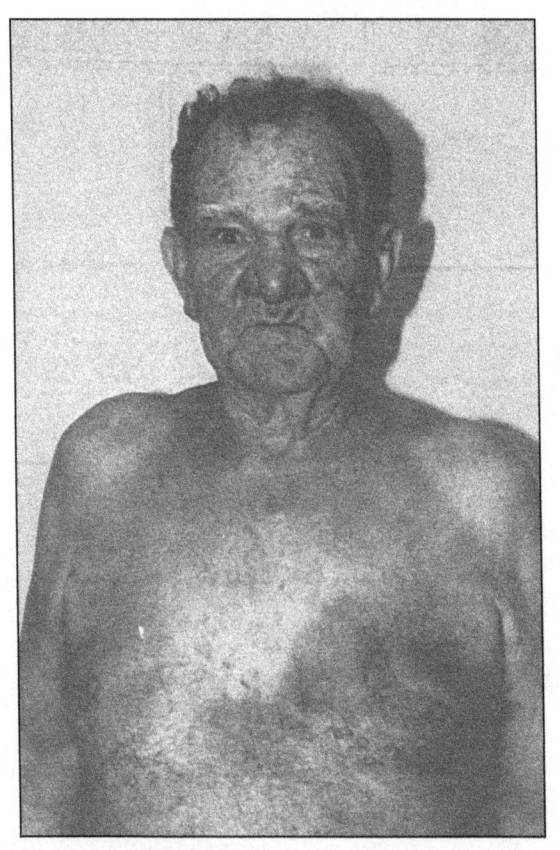

A dissipated Lawrence Singleton at the time of his arrest for the murder of Roxie Hayes. Police noted that there was blood on his chest.
Courtesy of Hillsborough County Sheriff's Office

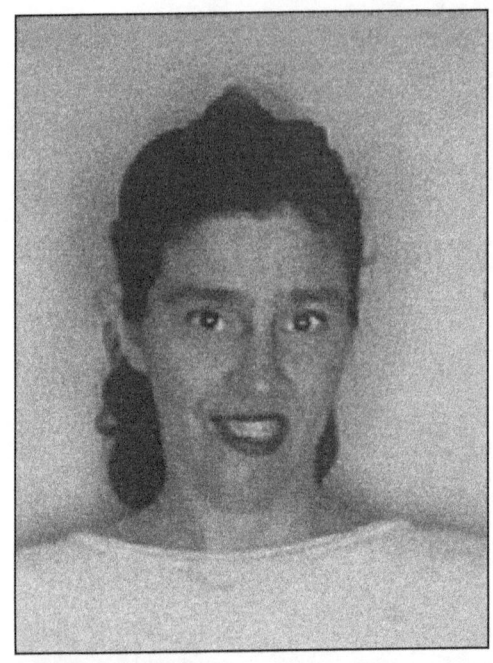

Roxanne "Roxie" Hayes, career prostitute, 1996. Courtesy of Hillsborough County Sheriff's Office

The Tampa house where Singleton stabbed Roxie to death.
Author's collection

The driveway of his Tampa home where Singleton tried to commit suicide just prior to his brutal murder of Roxie Hayes.
Author's collection

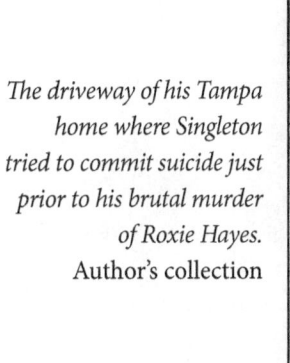

Mary Vincent, 15, just before her forearms were hacked off by Singleton in 1977.
Courtesy of *The Modesto Bee*

Police drawing of Singleton's Bay area home, created from description given by Mary Vincent under hypnosis.
Courtesy of Richard Breshears

Amazingly accurate police sketch of Mary Vincent's attacker as described by Vincent. Courtesy of Richard Breshears

The forensic x-rays of both parts of Mary Vincent's severed arm. The bone breaks matched almost exactly. Author's collection

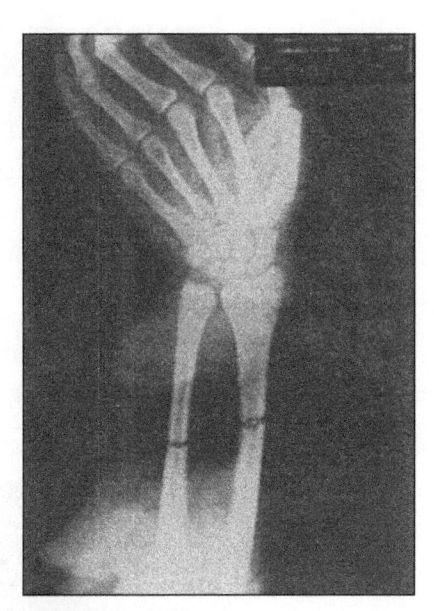

Aerial shot of the barren area and the culvert where Singleton left Vincent for dead. Courtesy of *The Modesto Bee*

The culvert where Singleton stuffed Mary Vincent after he cut off her forearms. Courtesy of *The Modesto Bee*

The coast in the San Francisco Bay Area where Vincent's severed forearm was found.

Vincent's severed hand and forearm as found by a fisherman.
Courtesy of *The Modesto Bee*

The air strip where Todd Meadows drove Mary Vincent to call the police after her vicious attack.
Courtesy of *The Modesto Bee*

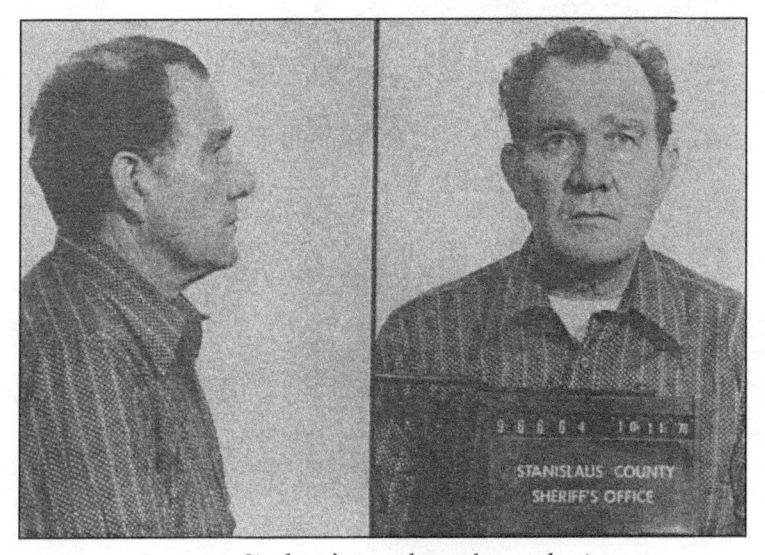

Lawrence Singleton's mug shot, taken at the time of his arrest for the attack on Vincent.
Courtesy of Hillsborough County Sheriff's Office

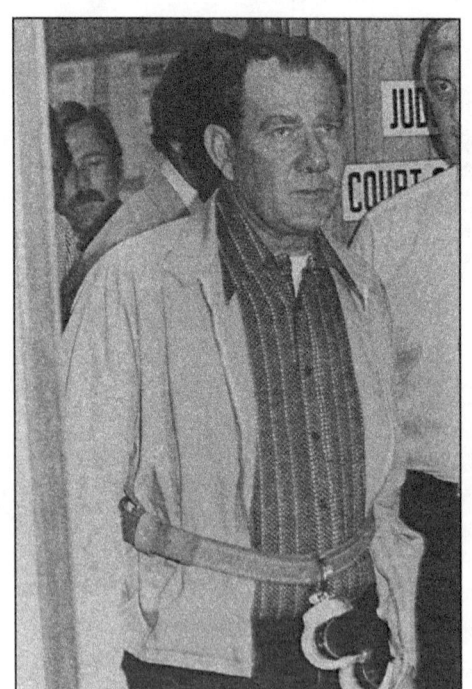

Vincent's family on their way to visit her during her recuperation from the assault.
Courtesy of
The Modesto Bee

Singleton arrived under heavy security for his arraignment in 1978.
Courtesy of
The Modesto Bee

Detective Richard Breshears (left) helping to convey evidence confiscated in Singleton's home. Courtesy of The Modesto Bee

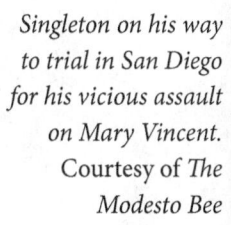

Singleton on his way to trial in San Diego for his vicious assault on Mary Vincent. Courtesy of The Modesto Bee

Mary Vincent holds up her newly fitted prosthetic arms in triumph. Courtesy of The Modesto Bee

Lawrence Singleton, 1986, after his release. Courtesy of The Modesto Bee

The living room of Singleton's Tampa home where Police found the dead body of Roxie Hayes. Investigators speculated that the rope would have been used to drag the body out of the house.
Courtesy of Hillsborough County Sheriff's Office

The autopsy revealed the deep wounds on Hayes's fingers from trying to protect herself from Singleton's deadly knife attack.
Courtesy of Hillsborough County Sheriff's Office

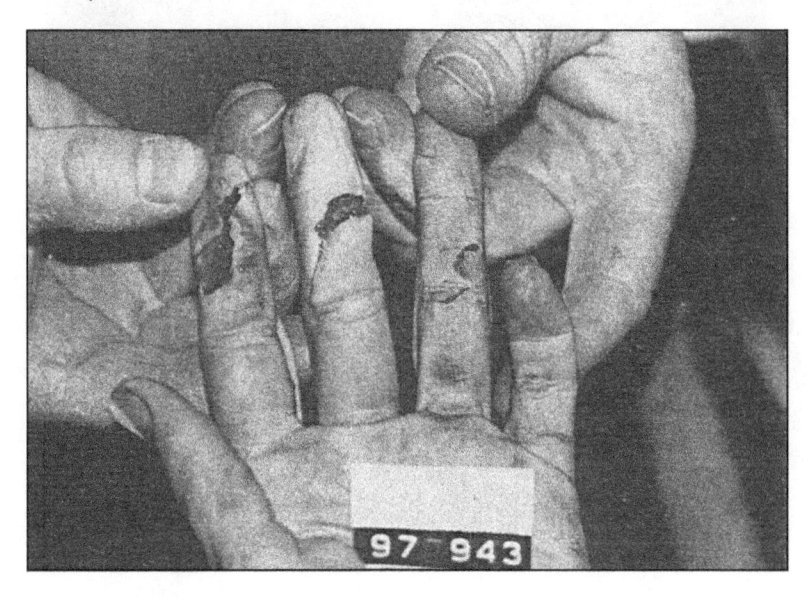

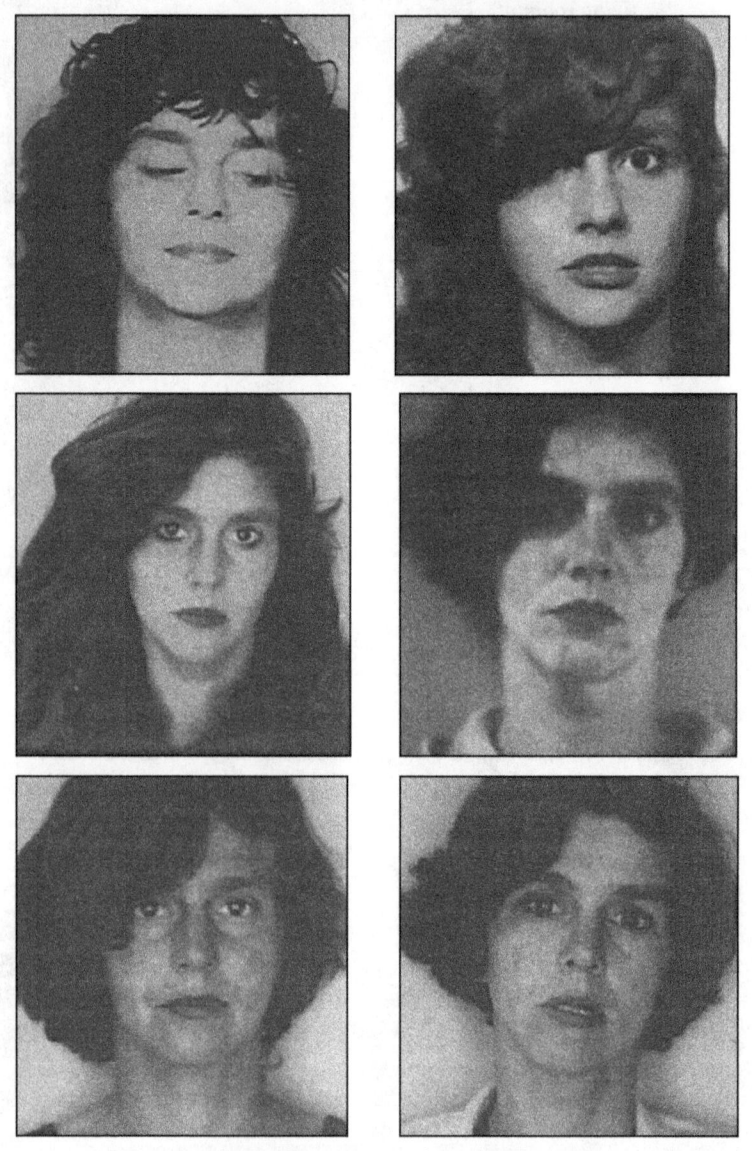

*Mug shots of Roxie Hayes for various counts
of prostitution from 1986–1995.*
Courtesy of Hillsborough County Sheriff's Office

FRED ROSEN

FROM OPEN ROAD MEDIA

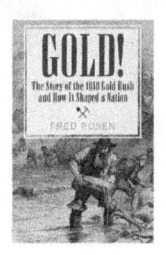

OPEN ROAD
INTEGRATED MEDIA

Find a full list of our authors and titles at www.openroadmedia.com

FOLLOW US
@OpenRoadMedia

EARLY BIRD BOOKS
FRESH DEALS, DELIVERED DAILY

Love to read?
Love great sales?

Get fantastic deals on bestselling ebooks delivered to your inbox every day!

Sign up today at
earlybirdbooks.com/book